Celtic Magic

Unlocking Druidry, Earth Magick, Irish Shamanism, Tree Magic, and Scottish Paganism

Your Free Gift (only available for a limited time)

Thanks for getting this book! If you want to learn more about various spirituality topics, then join Mari Silva's community and get a free guided meditation MP3 for awakening your third eye. This guided meditation mp3 is designed to open and strengthen ones third eye so you can experience a higher state of consciousness. Simply visit the link below the image to get started.

https://spiritualityspot.com/meditation

Contents

Introduction

Modern-day Wicca has its roots in Celtic magic, and many practices taught these days are derived from these ancient traditions. Druids were known to dabble in divination and mysticism, from various forms still known today. Engaging in hymns and chants, creating incantations, and writing and reciting blessings and curses are the foundations of Celtic magic and, more specifically, Wicca.

This type of magic has been practiced for over two thousand years, and now, thanks to the handy guide you have in your hands, modern Wiccans can feel even more connected to their shared past. This book provides an unprecedented thorough yet comprehensible introduction to the transformative powers of practical magic. You will learn to harness your natural abilities while delving deeper into ancient traditions and honoring the work of so many who came before us. This book also covers the Celts' history and how their traditions influence us today.

The vibrant traditions, myths, and the magic of this uniquely beautiful part of Wales will be thoroughly covered in the following chapters. Turn the pages, and you'll discover the magical gods and goddesses whose presence is still felt today and the spirits whose magic forms the foundational vibrations that continue to carry the Wiccan religion. Various rituals are elucidated, and you will feel closer than ever to the divine energy of nature. You will learn to work with spells, invocations, and magical tools, made newly accessible in these pages but whose histories are derived from authentic Celtic resources.

Celtic magic retains its belief system and practices entirely unique to the Welsh region. Of course, the contemporary practice of Wicca draws plenty of inspiration from the Celtic systems of magic, and non-Celtic traditions, such as Teutonic, the Greco-Roman, and even Native American. However, these blends confuse contemporary practitioners and mislead people as to how these particular systems originated. In this guide, the Celtic sensibility and particular forms of magic will be studied within their specific cultural context, and no watered-down versions will be included.

Ultimately, reviving ancient folk traditions, practices, stories, and histories is about keeping an important legacy alive and its heart beating. Other narratives about the Celts and their magic observe them with the distant anthropologist's gaze, effectively "othering" the subject and flattening their characteristics with little regard for the specificity of its history. This book aims to do the complete opposite and provide a deeply immersive experience for the reader. If you're a new practitioner in the world of magic or someone who wants to learn more about this unique religion and practice, this book is for you. Other guides these days too much on parables and prettified stories. While there is always room for that, this book provides a more straightforward introduction to the fascinating Celts' magical practices and explores the ways they continue to influence contemporary magic.

Chapter 1: Celtic Magic Basics

It's essential to understand where the tradition of this magic comes from - the ancient Celts - to understand Celtic magic. If you've never heard of them, don't worry. This chapter discusses everything to know about the ancient Celts and Celtic magic basics and Celtic Neopaganism, Celtic Wicca, and Celtic magic today. By the time you've finished reading the chapter, you'll have answers to any questions you may have had on the topic.

The Ancient Celts

"Celt" is the collective name for several groups of ancient people who lived in Europe and Anatolia. Their related family Celtic languages link them, hence the use of the word "Celt." The Celts consisted of:

- Brits
- Gaels
- Gauls
- Galatians
- Celtiberians and many more

Additionally, these groups had several cultural similarities, which helped connect them.

They are believed to have a history tracing back to 1200 BC, if not longer. However, the word "Keltoi" was first used in Greek sources in the 5th century BC. In the 1st century BC, Julius Caesar reported that the Gauls referred to themselves as Celts, indicating that the tribes adopted the Greek name sometime between the four centuries. The modern word "Celt" was first used in the 1700s.

During their heyday, the Celts occupied territories stretching from Spain to the Black Sea, making them the largest ethnic group in ancient Europe. However, it's important to remember that the Celts were a collection of disparate tribes united by a common language, family, and cultural customs rather than a single kingdom. It makes tracing a single history of the Celts challenging.

The Celts thrived because of the vast territory they inhabited. For example, while the Roman Empire was expanding through Europe, the Celts on the islands of Ireland and Great Britain remained relatively isolated and grew as a culture. While Julius Caesar and his successors launched a targeted battle to destroy the Celts in Mainland Europe, their attempted invasion of Britain remained unsuccessful, making the islands a haven for the surviving Celts. Therefore, the

Celtic cultural traditions are particularly prevalent in Ireland and the United Kingdom and the source of modern Celtic Neopaganism.

Though sources from the Greeks and Romans refer to the ancient Celts as barbarian warriors, it would be a mistake to think of them as such. The recorded barbaric nature of the Celts due to a combination of propaganda and war - the Roman Empire, in particular, benefitted from portraying their enemies negatively, as it made their armies more likely to fight and justified the war against the Celts. Additionally, when Caesar decided to abandon the invasion of Britain, the decision was justified in part by referencing the "barbarity" of the Celts and juxtaposing it against the "civilized" Mediterranean world.

However, there is significant evidence of the intricacy and richness of Celtic culture. For example, ancient Celtic burial mounds prove their skills as metalworkers and jewelers and the complexities of Celtic social culture. While Greek and Roman sources describe the Celts as "excessive drinkers," discoveries of burial mounds show that drinking was a way for tribes to strengthen allyship, and the presentation of alcohol (and other elements of a grand feast) was a sign of a good leader's generosity.

The Celts were also known for their intricate bronze and iron weaponry, which included highly personalized swords and shields with motifs tailored to each individual. These weapons helped them defeat the early Romans in the British Isles and established their reputation as fierce warriors. However, the detail of the weapons also shows they were often used for ritual purposes.

Celtic Languages

As mentioned above, one thing that tied disparate Celtic tribes together was a shared language family. Though the Celtic languages have evolved into many languages today, there were two main languages groups the ancient Celts likely spoke - Insular and Continental Celtic.

Continental Celtic has been extinct since about the 5th century AD, and the best-documented example can be found in Gaulish ancient documentation. Insular Celtic evolved into a range of languages, and some are still spoken today, including:

- Cumbrian (extinct)
- Breton (endangered but undergoing a revival)
- Cornish (recently revived)
- Welsh (still spoken today)
- Irish and Scottish Gaelic (still spoken today)
- Cornish (recently revived)
- Manx (recently revived)

The revival of ancient Celtic languages can be tied to opposition to British rule. The 19th and 20th centuries saw a revival of the Celtic identity in the British Isles (including Celtic religion, as we discuss later in this chapter) and was primarily driven by anger at British rule over other UK countries like Ireland, Wales, and Scotland. While the British government restricted the ancient Celtic languages, this embrace of Celtic identity also led to the revival of the languages and their use in everyday and formal situations.

Ancient Celtic Religion

While the Celts remain a fascinating subject of study to people around the world, the element of their culture serves as the biggest remains their religion and spiritual belief system. There is no "name" for the ancient Celtic religion, and some elements are shared with other contemporary belief systems, including:

- Polytheism
- Offerings to the gods
- A belief in the afterlife, characterized by leaving valuable and everyday items in the tombs of the deceased

With the Celtic people, there was no single unified religion shared by all the tribes. However, while primary gods, offerings, and places of worship may have differed from tribe to tribe, these disparate religions were extraordinarily similar in other ways, including:

- A reverence for the human head and a belief that it was the seat of the soul

- The belief that totems - especially animal totems like the stag and the boar - had a protective power

- Reverence for sacred sites, especially ones related to nature like groves, rivers, and springs

- Religious ceremonies that were, more often than not, led by Druids

- Religious and community rules were meant to be complied with and often ensured through the use of taboos for people who went against them.

There is a good chance that the ancient Celts practiced human sacrifice. However, human sacrifices were significantly rarer than animal sacrifices and offerings of other items, like food and weapons. Where human sacrifice was practiced, the sacrifice differed depending on the god the sacrifice was made. Some buried bodies discovered are thought to be local kings or people sacrificed by the Celts.

It should be noted that everything known of ancient Celtic religion today is based on surviving artifacts and the oral traditions passed on through centuries in closed communities. Druids and poets were frequently unwilling to commit sacred knowledge to write. Therefore, knowledge of Celtic magic and religious practices is from the Romans and Greeks, who extensively documented Celtic practices, and reconstructions based on existing Celtic artifacts. It's possible that many more Celtic artifacts were destroyed during the invasion of Celtic lands by the Roman and Germanic tribes. The existence of the Romanic counterparts of Celtic deities indicates Romans had a much broader knowledge of the nature and attributes of these deities than we can surmise from the artifacts existing today.

Most scholars agree that the Celts practiced a form of animism - a belief that all parts of the natural world had their own spirits. Some Celtic gods were local spirits. For example, the Irish Celtic goddesses Boann and Sioann were associated with Boyne and Shannon rivers, and The Morrígan was linked to the River Unius. Additionally, some gods and goddesses, like Artio (bear) and Epona (horse), are linked to animals.

Not only did the Celts associate their deities and spirits with elements of nature, but they also believed in the spiritual importance of these elements. According to the Celtic lore, these higher beings lived in mountain tops, trees, bodies of water - and when the time arose, they came out to assist people. The Celts often held their rituals at points where two major natural elements joined. These were the common areas where the inhabitants of the physical and supernatural worlds could communicate freely with each other.

In artwork that has survived the passage of time, Cernunnos, also known as "the horned god," is the best-known and most frequently depicted Celtic god. His role in the pantheon of gods remains veiled in mystery, although he is generally depicted in a seated position with stag antlers. Other major gods and goddesses include the healing goddess Brigid (known as Brigantia), the warrior god Lugh (known as Lugus and Lleu Llaw Gyffes), and the triple goddess Matrones. Triple deities were a relatively common phenomenon in Celtic religion. Some deities like Lugh and The Morrígan were often considered triple deities and individual figures, depending on the tribe and the religious tradition.

Ancient Celtic Religion and Magic

The Druids and the poets led the Ancient Celtic religion, and both groups were connected to magic.

The Druids were essentially the priests of the ancient Celtic religion and were tasked with linking humans and the gods. They were also the keepers of a community's history and respected for their knowledge of customs, traditions, and wisdom in all things.

They lead religious ceremonies, but this was only one part of their duties. They were also soothsayers who divined the future and interpreted natural events, made medicinal potions, and used sacred plants common people were not permitted to use (like mistletoe). Additionally, they were tasked with casting taboos (what we now call spells) on people who disobeyed religious and community rules.

As with ancient Celtic religion, knowledge of Druidic tradition comes from writings of Romans and Greeks. The Druids left little to no written sources for us to learn from. However, it's worth noting that the Celtic-based Roman written records contain the same elements as the ancient Celtic folk songs and oral legends passed down by the Druids, poets, and bards.

Becoming a druid was a complex procedure and could often take as many as 20 years of training. Some sources have Druids capable of:

- Producing snow storms
- Having power over the elements
- Creating illusions to fool enemies during wartime

Druids sometimes adopted specific postures while casting spells, but much of the magical power was in the actual words, which is why their extensive knowledge of these spells was so vital. It also explains the lack of written sources, as writing these spells down would allow others to understand and use their power.

Aside from Druids, knowledge of magic was also held by Celtic poets, especially in Ireland, known as the *fili*. Like the Druids, becoming a poet required extensive training, and poets were tasked with remembering numerous lengthy poems (sometimes hundreds). This extensive knowledge and memorization ability meant that poets were assigned as lore keepers for communities.

In Celtic Ireland, poets were seen and treated as people with a magical capacity; it was believed that poetry, or poetic expression, is intrinsically related to a form of magic or magical clairvoyance that gave poets unusual power in society. As mentioned above, spells and curses depended on the spoken word more than any gestures from the caster's side, and satirical poems spoken by a poet were often considered curses cast upon the person or persons being satirized in the poem.

It should be noted that poets were different from bards in Ireland. Bards were reciters of existing poems, while poets were artists with magical abilities who could create new poems. However, in Wales, poets and bards were interchangeable terms.

According to some Roman sources, a separate class of seers also existed, different from the Druids and poets. These seers were supposed to interpret natural events, like bird's flight, to tell the future. However, most sources combine the order of seers with the Druids.

Aside from codified magic from the Druids and the poets, there were instances of more "everyday" magic among the ancient Celts. The most significant of this "smaller" magic is using amulets. Amulets were charms believed to have the ability to ward off danger. They were designed for living people (and the dead) and were often found in women's and children's graves. Furthermore, talismans were a different class of magical items believed to bring luck to the wearer or owner.

Celtic Magic Today

Over time, Celtic societies underwent gradual Christianization (as did much of Europe). The last Celtic country to convert to Christianity was Ireland, but by the 5th-7th century AD, the Church relegated traditional Celtic practices to irrelevancy, and the poets and Druids were rebranded as demonic and pagan practitioners. To further discourage pagan practices, fairies and other natural spiritual guides were also transformed into malevolent entities by Christian priests.

However, Celtic religion and tradition survived in pieces and folklore around the Celtic countries. If the Celts couldn't worship their gods and goddesses openly, they converted them into heroes and heroines in legends passed on to the next generations. In fact, the Celtic oral tradition was so strong that these stories are nearly the same today as they were recorded in older sources.

Some rituals, particularly those thought to have healing properties, such as a pilgrimage to clootie wells, the practice of well dressing, and using wish trees, remained in use even during the height of Christianity. In some isolated parts of these countries, like the Inishkea Islands located off the coast of Ireland, Celtic rituals were practiced well into the 19th century.

Additionally, the 1900s saw a resurgence of interest in Celtic traditions and Celtic religion. As mentioned above, it was a way of resisting British rule over other countries in the United Kingdom, especially Scotland and Ireland. Since using many Celtic languages was either outlawed or severely discouraged and penalized, this period also saw a resurrection of interest in these languages.

Celtic Reconstructionist Paganism

Celtic Reconstructionist Paganism is perhaps the best-known approach to Celtic neopaganism and takes a Reconstructionist approach to the religion. It prioritizes historical accuracy over combining Celtic religion with other pagan traditions, common in Neo-Druidism and Celtic Wicca.

Celtic Reconstructionist Paganism originated from various modern pagan religions of the 1970s and 1980s and grew as a religion in the 1980s and 90s. Core parts of this tradition include studying and reviving Celtic languages and focusing on Celtic cultural activities, including music, dance, and even traditional martial arts.

Practitioners also focus on preserving important archeological and sacred Celtic sites like sites around the Hill of Tara and have engaged in protests to ensure their survival.

Rituals include:

- Acknowledging the realms of the land, sea, and sky.

- Using the fire of inspiration as a force that unites and binds these realms together.

- Maintaining altars and shrines to personal deities.

- Some practitioners also practice divination with the help of the traditional Ogham alphabet or through interpreting natural happenings like the movements of clouds and birds.

Celtic Wicca

Apart from Celtic Reconstructionist Paganism, the other well-known version of Celtic neopaganism is Celtic Wicca. This subset of modern Wiccan practice combines Wiccan beliefs with Celtic mythology.

Celtic Wiccans believe the same basic customs as other Wiccans, including the Wiccan Rede and the Rule of Three. They also worship the divine Goddess and God. However, unlike traditional Wicca, Celtic Wicca is not duo-theistic. Celtic Wiccans also worship several other deities from Celtic mythology, with important deities including:

- Brigid

- Cerridwen

- Rosmerta

- Rhiannon

- Cernunnos (as mentioned above, Cernunnos is often known as the horned god. For Celtic Wiccans, he is frequently equated and combined with the divine male - the God)

- Lugh

It should be noted that how a person practices Celtic Wicca is often exceptionally personal. Many practitioners focus more on one aspect over the other, Wicca over Celtic religion, or vice versa. Celtic Wiccans who focus on the Celtic religion will often find the Wiccan Rede is incompatible with Celtic ethics of heroic mortality. Those who focus more on the Wicca aspect will incorporate the four elements into their spiritual traditions.

Celtic Wiccans generally celebrate the same eight Sabbats as other Wiccans do - the Wiccan Wheel of the Year and the Sabbats have origins in Celtic traditions, making it a core aspect of the Celtic Wiccan tradition. However, unlike Celtic Reconstructionist Paganism, Celtic Wicca remains a combination of two religious traditions rather than a movement focused on historical accuracy.

Neo-Druidism

As mentioned above, another Celtic Neopagan tradition is Neo-Druidism. It is, essentially, a revival of Celtic Druidism and its origins in the interest in Celtic religion during the 18th and 19th centuries.

During the 18th-century Romanticist movement in Britain, interest in the ancient Celts peaked. Early Neo-Druids aimed to imitate the original Druids and revive the Celtic culture.

As discussed above, there is little extant information about the original Druids, especially in primary sources. Due to this issue, Neo-Druidism was modeled on secret societies like Freemasonry and used Druids as a symbol of the indigenous spirituality of ancient Britain. There were several societies of Neo-Druids, and some were - and remain - purely cultural in nature. However, others have moved towards a more spiritual aspect, including nature worship, a belief in Awen (the idea of divinity and the Deity's spirit), goddess worship, and ancestor veneration.

It should be mentioned that, like Celtic Wicca, Neo-Druidism is not historically accurate. While modern Druids participate in ceremonies and rituals, celebrate during the Sabbats, and engage in several other magical practices, such as herbalism and divination, this does not mean they accurately represent ancient Druidic orders.

Even Celtic Reconstructionist Paganism is ultimately a Reconstructionist approach towards ancient Celtic religion. The lack of primary sources makes accurate replication of the religion challenging at the best of times, and practitioners have had to innovate their versions of the religion.

If you're interested in learning more about Celtic magic, including how to practice ogham divination, use tree magic, and conduct Celtic rituals, you're in the right place. The next chapter will detail the gods and goddesses you will encounter as part of the Celtic pantheon. You'll be introduced to Celtic magic in Ireland and Scotland, given a better understanding of druidism and the way of the druid, and learn much more. Keep reading to learn all you need to know about the Celtic religion.

Chapter 2: The Celtic Pantheon

Celtic mythology is always enchanting, and when we explore it, we are not talking about a particular group that happened to dominate a specific realm. Instead, we are focusing on exploring the dynamic culture of the Celtic era that strongly influenced many regions, including the Danube, Portugal, Ireland and more. Since it's multifarious, since the Celtic mythology as we know it today has numerous borrowed tales and traditions, an important note is to remember that their gods and goddesses have associated deities or cognates, depending on the region. For instance, Lugus, as it was known in the region of Gaul, was also known as Lugh in Ireland. Let's explore the most important gods and goddesses of the majestic Celtic Era.

1. Dana: Goddess of Nature

She is one of the oldest of all the ancient gods in Celtic mythology. Dana is known by many names such as Annan, Danu, Anu and is often recognized as the primordial mother goddess. This Celtic goddess is portrayed as a stunning and wise woman, deeply linked with nature and the spiritual essence of natural entities. Dana also stands for regeneration, prosperity, wisdom and death.

This goddess played a significant role in Celtic mythology and was regarded as the divine mother of Tuatha De Danann (the people of goddess Dana). Tuatha De Dannan was one of the greatest pantheons from Pre-Christian Ireland and considered a supernatural tribe or race of Celtic gods.

How to Honor Today?

Select a time when you can focus on the honoring ritual, about half an hour or, at the very least, chalk out 10 minutes. The best times are before sunrise or post-sunset, but you can select any time in the day if these don't suit you. Ideally, the ritual to worship Dana should be performed outdoors, but indoors will do just fine if you are uncomfortable with this. You will have to repeat the ritual basics, including grounding yourself, deep breathing to center and then going through the steps of a purification ritual. Now you are ready to connect with the deity Danu. You can call her with any name or title that feels closer to your heart. The invocation needs to be sincere instead of long-winded, and you must make an offering (wine, water, or ale). Afterward, sit quietly and visualize her. When she appears before you (perhaps you hear her or receive a sign), greet her, let her communicate with you, and listen with respect. Once you feel the communication has concluded, pour another offering to the goddess and drink some yourself. It is important not to rush the ritual and be polite and patient.

2. Dagda: Chief of All Gods

He happens to be an important fatherly deity and is called a cheerful god and chief of all the Celtic gods. Dagda is a deity linked with all the nourishing and earthly aspects, including fertility, masculine strength, weather, and agriculture. But this is not all; Dagda's divine powers were thought to encompass wisdom, knowledge, Druidry, and magic as well. It often intrigues the reader to learn about the physical appearance of deity Dagda as a simple and plump man who has aged. He is often represented wearing a rustic and old tunic. However, the one interesting element you will always see in the pictures or representations of the deity Dagda is the Lorg Mór (great staff or the club) with magical powers. His magical staff could resurrect the dead or bring death upon several simultaneously. You would notice the simple and nurturing deity, Dagda, never without his magical cauldron and a big ladle, known as "*coire ansic.*" The cauldron represented his connection with the magical, mysterious and surreal aspects of this world, while the ladle was a symbolic representation of Dagda's immense power over food, sustenance and abundance in general. He also had many lovers, including the goddess Morrigan.

How to Honor Today?

To celebrate the fatherly Dagda, simply make different offerings to him, like porridge or oat bannocks, ale, and butter to the fire while performing the ritual. Place different bounty and abundance symbols on the altar, including produce you have grown, and load a big cauldron with home-baked food and home-grown vegetables. Another way to honor him is to make food donations to the local food bank or be generous and hospitable to others around you.

3. Morrigan: Goddess of Fate

According to Celtic mythological folklore, the goddess of fate is also recognized as a mysterious deity known by the name of *Morrigu*. Moreover, she seems to be an ominous figure linked with terrifying wars and mysteries of fate. Morrigan was thought to have prophetic powers of premonitions of doom. There are several interpretations of her name in history that are quite intriguing, but one of the most interesting is the "phantom queen," as she was able to change her form or shape and would usually turn into a crow.

As mentioned earlier, Morrigan has been linked with foretold doom, and her reputation as an ominous deity stands true, as according to the stories, she lured soldiers to the frenzy of the battlefield. She is also popular among the believers as the deity of sovereignty and was considered a protector for the land and believers. When you peruse through the history of Morrigan, it is interesting to note the connection that has been established with other deities, including Nemain, Badb, and Macha. Not only this, but Morrigan also shared an interesting tryst with Dagda on Samhain.

How to Honor Today?

You must first get to know this deity in-depth, so spend ample time studying her and how she manifests in different cultures. Prepare a dedicated altar for her and place drawings or a statue of Morrigan. Use black or red candles, an altar cloth, and decorative deer and crows. Also, keep a bowl of water. You can perform shapeshifting shamanic rituals and practice meditation or shamanic drumming.

4. Lugh: Warrior God

He is the warrior god, known by Lugus, Lugos, Lugh Lámhfhada (Lugh of the Long Arm), and Lleu Llaw Gyffes (Lleu of the skillful hand), and represented as a powerful, courageous deity. He is among the most respected and celebrated deities that have been famous for their mesmerizing warrior persona and youthful appearance. However, one must not be deceived by the youthful appearance of deity Lugh, as his power was unmatchable. Lugh was the one deity who slayed the chief of Formorii, a formidable one-eyed Balor (an enemy of the tribe of gods, i.e., the Tuatha De Danann). An interesting irony or a twist of fate was that even though Lugh was heralded as the Balor slayer, he was one among Balor's descendants. Lugh was linked with lynxes, thunderstorms, raves and was known as Samildanach (skilled in all arts). Some various interesting mythical stories and folklores connect Lugh and Cu Chulainn (who was an Irish hero) as father and son. It is worth mentioning that Cu Chulainn is quite similar to Hercules/Heracles and Rostam. The folklores and mythology have a weird and spellbinding interconnection that does not cease to amuse the scholars to date.

How to Honor Today?

To honor the god of war, Lugh brings bread, grains, corn, or other harvest symbols as offerings. Before starting the honoring ritual for Lugh, spend time taking a personal inventory of your strengths, talents, goals, etc. Add items that speak about your talents onto the altar. You will need one candle to symbolize Lugh and place it in the center of the altar. When you light the candle, take another second to refresh all your life achievements. Make an incantation honoring Lugh and introducing yourself as a skilled devotee. Take pride in your skills (but don't be impolite or snobbish because you are speaking to a deity). Afterward, ask about the thing you want to improve. Make another offering, conclude the ritual with gratitude, and spend a few more minutes reflecting on your abilities.

5. Brigid: Triple Goddess of Healing

The triple goddess, Brigid, is quite popular for her reputation as a spring goddess and the deity of smithcraft as well as healing. She is also strongly associated with some peculiar brooding attributes of Morrigan. As far as, Celtic mythology and folklore go, Brigid is recognized as the daughter of the deity Dagda and has been an esteemed member of the divine tribe of deities, the Tuatha De Danann. One striking aspect of Goddess Brigid is her strong connection with the domestic animals, including oxen, boars, sheep. These animals would loyally warn the goddess of any upcoming calamity. This goddess was generally venerated as the poet, the healer, and the smith. In other words, she may even have been considered a triple deity.

How to Honor Today?

Start by learning more and reading mythical texts about her. The next step is to set up an altar for her, as Brigid loves having a dedicated small space in her followers' homes. She is a goddess of the hearth, so the kitchen seems the perfect spot. You can decorate the altar with a picture or statue of her, a glass of water, and a candle. It's as simple as that. While speaking to her, don't forget to light a candle purely to connect deeply with Brigid. You can also honor her by acknowledging other elements, like water. All you have to do is visit a nearby spring or well or any natural water body that would serve this purpose. Simply show your gratitude and humbly ask for healing your soul, body, and mind.

6. Epona: Guardian Goddess of Horses

Epona is considered the female deity and serves as the protector of horses, mules, and donkeys. This Celtic goddess is also linked with fertility. Roman Empire cavalrymen venerated goddess Epona, and they favored her strongly. Goddess Epona was quite popular among the Equites Singulares Augusti, who were the Imperial Horse Guards. These guards were the counterparts in Praetorian Guards, and according to some stories, Epona was the one who actually instilled a spirit of inspiration in Rhiannon. The stories about mythical Welsh Rhiannon, who was also famously recognized for her tenacity and labeled as the otherworld's lady, are strongly linked with goddess Epona.

Epona's symbol is a horse since she is crowned as the goddess who protects animals. She is sometimes shown carrying corn in her lap or a goblet and is believed to inspire providence, love, and fertility. She can also help in situations when you need more authority.

How to Honor Today?

If you want to show her regard, eat corn and leave roses as an offering for her. You can also use rose incense or rose petals. If that is not an option for you, use sandalwood incense. The color most often associated with her is white, so don't forget to grab a candle of that color. She is a goddess linked to various aspects of our lives. You can ask her to fulfill your dreams, and she blesses the ones we see while asleep. But she is also the goddess of ambition and hope. So, if you want to manifest your dreams and seek protection, she is the goddess you should honor today. She is depicted as a caregiver, so pray to her for the protection of children, families, and pregnant women.

7. Belenus: The Sun God (Beli Mawr, Bel, and Belenos)

The Sun God was one of the most time-honored and idolized gods in Celtic history. He was often shown to be riding the sky in a majestic, divine horse chariot. He is also sometimes depicted as throwing thunderbolts, riding a single horse or using the mystical wheel as a shield. Romans linked him with Apollo (also known as the god of light). Therefore, Belenus is also cheered for his regenerative and healing powers.

How to Honor Today?

You can honor Belenus by offering ritualistic offerings similar to other gods and goddesses by first learning more about him before moving on to the purifying and grounding rituals. The general offerings typical of Belenus include terra-cotta horses and stone-carved swaddled infant statues.

8. Aonghus: God of Love

The name of this deity is often translated as "true vigor," and he is popularly linked with love. Like the deity, Lugh, Aonghus, or Aengus, is another deity who is celebrated for his youthful appearance. He is also popularly worshipped for the connection with spirits or themes of love and poetry. According to the mythological stories, Dagda and Bionn (the goddess of rivers) were supposedly his parents. As far as the folklore goes, Dagda and Bionn were involved in an illicit relationship, and as a consequence, Bionn got pregnant. However, Dagda tried to hide her pregnancy and the truth behind their illicit relationship by magically controlling the weather. The mythology narrates that Dagda froze or halted the sun for a whole nine months, and that's how the deity Aengus was born in a matter of a day! Despite the peculiar history of his parents, the god Aonghus grew up to be a lively deity full of love and affection for the creatures around him. You would see his representations with four birds always around him. Later on, Aengus tricks his father (Dagda) in an attempt to confiscate and rule over the divine tribe of Tuatha De Danann's Bru na Boinne. However, he was crowned as the deity of love, primarily because of his story. Aengus fell in love with Caer Ibormeith, who he saw in a dream. He eventually found and married her.

How to Honor Today?

Start with the same rituals of honoring and offering the gods and first learn more about him to connect with him on a deeper level. The prayer to Aengus should include his praise. Afterward, share what you are grateful for and ask him humbly for the things you need guidance for.

9. Taranis: The God of Thunder

Taranis was one of the gods among the triad of Celtic gods (along with Esus and Toutatis) and was called the god of thunder. This trait is particularly interesting because he was often compared to the god Jupiter and Zeus. The portraits or illustrations of Taranis often represent hum with a lightning bolt, and he looks physically similar to god Zeus. Another worth noticing thing is that Taranis was associated with fire (sky or air). He was shown in pictures, holding the solar wheel.

How to Honor Today?

There are several ways you can honor Taranis and express your devotion and dedication to this god. One way is to find lightning blasted oak and carry a piece of it with you. Another is to keep dried acorns and oak leaves with you in a mini sachet. When you are about to perform a ritual outdoors for Taranis, always make an offering to seek good weather. Making a fire-offering is recommended. Also, light a candle and offer a prayer to Taranis during lightning or thunder, showing your subservience to him. Another important detail to remember is to conclude the ritual by making the second offering showing your thanks.

10. Ogma: God of Eloquence

Deities that are linked with languages are not often seen in ancient folklore. This deity serves as an exception to the general rule because Ogma is the god of eloquence. Some stories represent the physical resemblance between Ogma and

Hercules. If you observe the depictions of Ogma, there are amber or gold-colored chains that are linked to his believers through his tongue. He was also an important character in the Garlic mythological tales. He invented the Ogham, which was an ancient writing system in Ireland. He was famously labeled as a deity of Knowledge.

How to Honor Today?

To honor Ogma, start on the path to knowledge, and the best beginning is to gather as much information about him as possible. If you perform a ritual to show your dedication and praise to Ogma, the altar should be set in a specific way. As the god of eloquence, offer a knowledgeable asset piece or make an equivalent offering. Spreading knowledge or wisdom is also an indication of dedication toward Ogma.

11. Cernunnos: Lord of All Things Wild

He happens to be one of the most imposing and impressive of all the Celtic gods because he was the deity of everything wild. Cernunnos was given the "Horned One" title and frequently linked with forests, animals, and fertility in Celtic polytheistic mythology. In Celtic mythology, he is reported as the son of deity Lugh and struggled to ensure the survival of wild animals and woods. His depictions often mirror all the associated characteristics. He has quite conspicuous antlers on his head and poetic epithets and represents the fatherly masculine energy of mother earth. He goes through the cycles of death and life; after death, he was reborn and impregnated by the goddess of Beltane. Therefore, he was not only born through the earth but also played an important role in fertilizing it. However, this interpretation is quite a new one associated with Cernunnos. His weapons were made of natural materials, including the tree's roots.

How to Honor Today?

Offer brown ale, cider, roasted rabbit, fruit punch, bone carvings, acorns, toadstools, green candles, boar hide, and flower fragrances. Like other deities, an essential aspect of honoring him is to learn more about him to get closer to him. However, nature is a key component for honoring Cernunnos. You can honor Cernunnos by offering dedicated ritualistic offerings by purifying, grounding, and visualizing while waiting for the god of all wild things to respond.

The Celtic mythology does not conclude with merely the above few deities. Many other gods and goddesses can also be included as relevant. Each deity has its unique attributes, and to show your devotion, you must honor each deity bearing this in mind.

Chapter 3: Celtic Magic in Ireland and Scotland

People without a deeper understanding of Celtic mythology often assume that Celtic magic is similar to Wicca and many other forms of Neopaganism practices. In reality, this couldn't be further from the truth, and nothing illustrates this better than Ireland and Scotland's unique Celtic magic practices.

Apart from having a history that dates back to 400 AD, the Celtic representation of the universe is based on nature, while, for example, Wicca relies on the four elements. The belief system of most modern

Pagans encourages using magic solely for healing and protection and never for harm. The Ancient Celts were mighty warriors who saw nothing wrong with harming someone if it meant their survival. This made it possible to occupy Ireland and Scotland, creating new territory to spread their beliefs. The most important characteristic differentiating Irish and Scottish Paganism from other forms is polytheism. This is another element leftover from the Ancient Celtic beliefs system, of which every god and goddess has its unique origin and function in the universe. While Wicca and similar modern Pagan practitioners often recognize the existence of multiple deities, these are said to be descendants of one god. This ideology is probably due to the mixed origins of these belief systems.

Celtic Magic in Ireland

Ireland is an island, isolating itself from the rest of the world. Due to this, there wasn't anything that could influence the spread of ancient pagan beliefs. Moreover, the practices of Ireland quickly evolved. First, it had to blend in with folk magic, also based on finding power in nature, and later Christianity, which was a much lengthier process. Nevertheless, this taught the Irish Celts a great lesson. They learned that sacred places could not be created. They could only be found, and once found, they did everything to keep it.

In Irish pagan mythology, birth, death, and rebirth are always intertwined, representing the elements of the same cycle. All creatures found themselves in three different realms, this world, the underworld, and the otherworld. The latter is often tied to the Tuatha Dé Danann, Ireland's well-known ancient Celtic tribe. According to legend, the "otherworld" was created as a world running in parallel to ours, so those banished from this world could continue living there. Deities and other elemental beings populate it. Using meditation and journeying, traveling between the realms is possible and often advised if one is seeking guidance. Practitioners typically do this with the necessary skills for gathering and sharing sacred wisdom in either realm.

The arrival of Christianity brought on the most substantial shift in the Irish Paganic practices. The priests took over the role of the Druids, causing their followers to change beliefs too. However, many Druids retained their pure Pagan beliefs, despite converting to Christianity or becoming priests.

Tuatha Dé Danann

The Tuatha Dé Danann (the People of the Goddess Danu) was one of the first Celtic tribes to take root in Ireland. Their gods were called Eriu and are still used as the name for Ireland in Celtic Pagan circles. Upon arrival at the Irish coastline, the Tuatha Dé Danann burned their boats, showing their absolute determination to take over this new land. After winning the battle with the ruler, the Fir Bolg, they succeeded and successfully ruled Ireland for over 200 years. Despite the sheer dominance they overtook Ireland with, the Tuatha were quite civilized. Their culture was admired by the conquered, and soon their skills and treasures became the source of tales still told today. According to these tales, the Tuatha Dé Danann possessed four talismans, and each was a testament to great power.

The four talismans were:

> 1. The Stone of Fal signaled when a true King of Ireland was standing on it.

2. The Sun God Lugh, with the ever-accurate slingshot.

3. The Magic Sword of Nuadha, which only inflicted mortal injuries.

4. The Cauldron of Dagda provided an endless supply of sustenance for the warriors.

Despite their arsenal and divine powers, the two-century rule of the Tuatha Dé Danann came to an end when the mortal Melesians defeated them. They were consigned to live underground and later to the magical otherworld but eventually took over a new role as the bearer of the fairies. They became known as the *people of the mound*, Aes sidhe or Aos Sí.

Aos Sí

Living in the otherworld, the Aos Sí are depicted in different forms. These mystical beings are sometimes described as elf-like creatures hidden from human eyes. In other depictions, they resemble tiny fairies. The latter is the modern characterization of Irish fairy folk, which in the case of Aos Sí, is the least accurate. Even though this interpretation seems to be the most popular, it's not reflected in descriptions provided by the oral sources available from ancient times. Most Irish tales describe them as tall as humans, fair, and beautiful.

They can cross between the two realms and often visit the mounds of Ireland, where they can be seen doing either mischief or good deeds. They must be treated with great respect to appease them, and regular offerings must be made to them. Since they have always been more advanced than mortals, they rarely show interest in humans who have learned to share their land with them.

In addition, modern pop culture often describes fairies as magical creatures with a penchant for good-natured trickery. However, according to Celtic lore, these creatures aren't always so benevolent. Some examples of malicious Aos Sí are the fairy vampire maiden, Leanan Sídhe, the headless horseman, Dullahan, an evil Leprechaun, Far Darrig, and the Bean Sídhe, or banshee (as it's known by its modern name.) The Aos Sí are often used in Irish mythology to answer something that cannot otherwise be explained. Natural catastrophes, diseases, birth deformities or even a simple case of bad luck could be attributed to them.

Legends about Aos Sí often have a recurring motif that emphasizes the importance of warding them off. Protective charms, wearing clothes inside out, and certain foods can keep these creatures away from people and animals. Since they are known to emerge from the otherworld through specific locations, one can avoid being led astray by avoiding these areas.

Tír na nÓg

The home of Aos Sí (and many other creatures) is said to be a magical place where time stands still, and no death, illness, or other mishaps happen. This part of the otherworld is located just outside the human realm. The only way to reach it is by using magic, which is how many have managed to find the pathway to cross. Some are taking this path searching for the eternal youth Tir na nOg offers, while others merely want answers to questions concerning their life in the human realm. According to Celtic lore, Tir na nOg (known as the land of youth) is home to many heroes whose fates were tied to this place.

A popular tale depicts the story of Oisin, a young Irish warrior who fell in love with Niamh, the daughter of the king of Tir na nOg. Niamh helped Oisin reach the magical land, where they lived happily together for three hundred years. However, Oisin missed Ireland, and Niamh eventually sent him back to his homeland. When he arrived, he realized that while time stood still in the otherworld, many years had passed in his own realm. His loved ones were long gone, and their home was abandoned. Deciding to go back to Tir na nOg, he started his journey when he noticed a stone he wanted to take with him. When he tried to pick it up, he fell, and time instantly caught up with him being over 300 years old meant he had crossed his lifetime. However, he was now at peace.

Irish Celtic Shamanism

Shamanism, in general, refers to a practice of reconnecting with nature as a form of experiencing divine consciousness. During their mystical journey, shamans extend a spiritual connection toward the outside world and their consciousness at the same time. Irish Celtic Shamanism is rooted in the spiritual energy of this land. It's an ancient tradition honoring the archetypes of the Celtic pantheon and sacred sites known from the oral shamanic lineages and tales of Celtic Ireland.

Through the practices of Irish Celtic Shamanism, you can learn to travel to the world of Spirit and retrieve the knowledge needed for guidance, healing, or divination. At the same time, the contemporary version often focuses on bringing you closer to nature and yourself. Taking this path will allow you to emerge from the experience as an empowered version of yourself who seeks the universal truth and isn't afraid to experience life to the fullest.

The terms "healing" and "retrieval" are interchangeable in the Irish (Gaelic) language, indicating that by revealing the hidden parts of yourself – or *retrieving* them, you can heal and become whole again. When all the damaged parts are recovered, you become a fighter instead of a bystander, or worse, a victim. In Irish Celtic Shamanism, there is no difference between the sacred vision of the soul and the love and compassion that come from the hearth. This is why it's so liberating to adopt the Celtic way of life, even in these modern times. By connecting to nature, we can recharge our spiritual energy to fill our entire day with positive intention. A strong intent, in turn, opens our hearts so we can perceive the meaning of life.

As you become more attuned to yourself, you will experience more powerful spiritual energies flowing towards you from nature. Your perception of the world starts to shift to a new insightful realm. Like it did in ancient times, Irish Celtic Shamanism is still a path that takes you on new adventures and allows you to forge connections to all the life forms that exist on this earth.

Celtic Magic in Scotland

While all historical evidence shows that Scottish Paganism has the same roots as its Irish counterpart, there are some notable differences between the two belief systems. Even though the Celts invaded Scotland shortly after taking over Ireland, the different geographical locations caused a significant divergence. Being connected to the mainland meant many other religions and practices influenced Scotland. For example, the nature-based folk had a substantial bearing on the Scottish Paganism development. Therefore, Pagans in Scotland came to respect nature as a sacred source of life. Human beings represent only a part of the whole and must learn how to co-exist peacefully with animals, plants, and every other living and non-living thing that exists around them. According to paganism, birth, growth, and death are interconnected and often carry spiritual meanings. Death is only a transitional phase in a person's life cycle, and it always leads to a new existence when the person is fully reincarnated.

In Scottish Paganism, even the deities are viewed as a manifestation of nature. The various divinities can take many different forms. Their gods and goddesses can send messages in many different ways, but the delivery is almost always connected to nature. They show up in animals, plants, and even human forms, particularly in dreams. Goddesses are thought to have a particular affinity to show up in the various elements of nature, so they are often held in much higher esteem. If one is looking for spiritual truth, they are much more likely to receive it from a goddess. The use of magical symbolism is one of the primary characteristics of Scottish Paganism, as is the case with its Irish counterpart.

The Sìth

Scottish Pagans have a very deep relationship with their land, evident in the traditional (ancient Gaelic) names they use for landmarks and events related to them. This is the result of honoring their ancestors buried in those lands. They believe they can maintain a relationship with the dead through the land. Similar to the Irish pagan belief system, the Scottish also recognize the existence of the otherworld. But the ancestor's spirits live on and provide guidance when needed.

However, according to most myths, the otherworld is also populated by many other creatures, including the Síth. These creatures are similar to Aos Sí from Irish Pagan mythology and are described as luminescent, fairy-like beings. The most notable difference is that while their Irish counterparts are believed to have mostly neutral dispositions, the Síth is almost described as malevolent creatures. They are said to lure humans in with their music, only to harm them. They can appear as cats, dogs, snakes, and ugly humans, representing danger for children and those unfamiliar with their lore.

According to another myth, the Síth are descendants of humans who lived dishonorable lives. As the other dead spirits living in the otherworld can communicate with the living, so can the Síth, except they always have an ulterior motive. If someone wants to communicate with them, they must understand the risk and must be prepared to bargain. Otherwise, the Síth will seek to harm whoever they encounter.

Scottish Pagans have learned how to communicate with all spirits of nature, allowing them to understand and explore the realms behind theirs. This ideology is very different from modern magic practices, based on Celtic beliefs that have lost the true essence that lies in the heart of the Scottish Pagan way of life.

Cat Síth

One of the creatures in Scotland pagans have learned to be wary of is the Cat Síth. Although its size is closer to a larger dog, it has very distinctive catlike features, including the smooth black fur all over its body (hence the name Cat Síth, or cat-fairy). It is believed to haunt the Scottish Highlands and is often mistaken for other larger animals living in the mountains. According to tales, many hunters and warriors have lost their lives hunting down this mysterious creature. Other myths suggest that the Cat Sìth are witches with human features and shapeshift into cats. However, they can only do this nine times before remaining a cat forever - a reference to the concept of cats having nine lives.

Whether they are fairies or witches, the general opinion is that they are not to be trusted. They lure people in, harm or steal from them. If the Cat Sìth crosses over a corpse of the dead before the burial, they can steal the deceased's soul. Gods cannot claim the dead without their soul, meaning they cannot remain in the otherworld. To prevent the theft of their ancestral souls, the Scottish set up guards to watch over the body until it's buried. These guards were known as Feill Fadalach, and they were to draw the creature's attention away from the body with the usual methods of distracting a cat. They could play games with them, use catnip, riddles, and even music. It's also common knowledge that cats are drawn to warmth. Lighting fires near a body could attract the Cat Sìth to the area, so it is to be avoided as much as possible.

Cù-Sìth

Another malicious creature living in the otherworld was the *Cù-Sìth,* or fairy dog. With its intimidating size, dark green disheveled fur, and braided or coiled tail, the Cù-Sìth represents a truly terrifying picture. Like its cat counterpart, the fairy dog haunts the Highlands and is often mistaken for other, bull-sized animals. Most of the time, they hide in their homes, located in the crevices of the rocky mountainsides. They can only be noticed by their glowing eyes or when they suddenly appear in front of those crossing the mountain. Even when they roam around, they are stealthy hunters and only warn their prey from afar with their howls. Their appearance is believed to be a bad sign, as Cù-Sìth is also considered a forbearer of death and alarming news. A Cù-Sìth can take the soul of the dead to the afterlife after terrifying the poor victim to death. Those traveling the mountains are warned that if they hear one or two howls, they need to reach shelter before hearing the third one, as this is the last warning before the creature attacks.

There are also myths about the Cù-Sìth being the servant of the Daoine Sìth, the divine creatures fated to live in the underground fairy mound. They would ask the creatures to bring human souls for specific purposes. For example, women nursing children could provide milk for them, and their children were often used as bait to lure them out. To prevent them from being taken by the Cù-Sìth, these women and their children were locked up as soon as the howling was heard.

The Baobhan Sìth

Also known as the banshees of the pagan lore, the Baobhan Sìth are fairy-like creatures living outside human society. Keeping track of their every move, the Baobhan Sìth easily draws in their victims by inviting them to dance. Unlike banshees, succubi, and similar creatures from other cultures' myths, the Baobhan Sìth don't care much about staying young or powerful. However, their victims are almost always young people and are believed to have specific meanings. For one, this represents a bigger challenge when exhausting the victim with dance. When they see the victim is tired from the dance, they attack, cut their necks open with their long fingernails, and drink their blood. Young people have healthier and richer blood, and this is probably another reason for their choice of victims.

Highland warriors and hunters were particularly at risk of being lured in when roaming the mountains and forests. Due to the smell of blood from their kills, the Baobhan Sìth was drawn to the humans. They even used tricks like shapeshifting into wolves and other wild animals to stalk and lure in their prey. In another tale, the Baobhan Sìth shapeshift into women designed to entice the men, get close to them, and feed on them. These women could be recognized due to hooves instead of feet, which they tried to conceal under long dresses and skirts. Originally, they were also women, but once killed by the Baobhan Sìth, they turned into creatures.

Fortunately, these creatures also have weaknesses humans can use against them. As per a popular Scottish tale, horses and iron are the two main weapons used against the Baobhan Sith. According to this tale, a group of young hunters stopped to spend a night in an abandoned hunting lodge. To celebrate a successful day of hunting, they built a fire and made dinner.

As soon as they began to eat and drink, they heard a knock on the door. When they opened the door, they saw four beautiful women who claimed to be lost in the forest and asked if they could join the men and gain food and shelter from them. The hunters were more than happy to have female company and invited them in. When the women wanted to dance, the men willingly obliged. Before they realized what was happening, the women attacked them, revealing their long nails and hoofs.

One of the men had stepped away from the women at this very moment and stood by the door. Witnessing the death of his fellow hunters, he hurled an iron object toward the woman about to attack him and ran outside to the horses. He managed to kill the Baobhan

Sith when the iron hit, but the others were on his trail. However, as soon as he reached his horse, he noticed the creatures weren't coming closer to him. He stood among the horses until dawn when the women went back to their homes in the forest. After a quick look at the bloodless bodies of the clansmen, he went home to tell his clan what had happened and warned them of the dangerous creatures that lurk in the form of women.

Chapter 4: The Way of the Druid

While the Celts were known as great warriors, their elite formed a class of highly educated people responsible for maintaining their customs and order. Their wisdom played a fundamental part in shaping Celtic Paganism into the unique practice we know it to be. From this chapter, you will learn more about the beliefs of these distinguished Celtic groups called the Druids.

Who Are the Druids?

In ancient times, Druids were a group of Celts that enjoyed distinguished status in their society. They belonged to a highly educated class, with many responsible roles. Among them were teachers, judges, healers, and magicians possibly described as the equivalent of modern priests (men and women.) Despite this, the only evidence about their lives and roles in Celtic society comes from oral sources. What made them suitable for their roles was that their knowledge resulted from decades-long education. They were forbidden to write anything down, which meant all their knowledge had to be memorized. The early evidence of Druidry comes from over 2000 years ago, while the most prominent work of this class was documented during the Iron Age. During this period, Druids were held in such esteem they were often granted more responsibility and liberty than the tribe leaders.

Druids were able to consult otherworldly spirits and predict the future, so they were often asked for advice on matters ranging from personal to the entire tribe. A particularly known method for providing guidance before making an important decision was pouring liquid between two spoons (one spoon had a hole, and the liquid was poured from above into the second spoon below). If their answer was unfavorable, they advised the tribe against making the decision in question.

Druids also issued judgments in legal matters and handed out penalties, such as banning the offender from sacrificial rituals. This was considered one of the gravest forms of punishment because it meant that the person could not receive the blessings, protection, or any other protection the rest of the tribe received by their sacrifice. Sometimes a matter would be decided by an assembly of Druids, all having equal merit in the decision-making. The Druids typically gathered in a sacred place to vote on important matters once a year.

Most of their offerings consisted of animal sacrifices, but some sources describe human sacrifices. According to these tales, when someone was wounded in battle and came close to dying, the Druids offered a human sacrifice to save them. This was done by building huge wickerwork, filling it with criminals, and burning them alive. Their lives were exchanged for the life of the wounded innocents.

They rarely engaged in physical combat and mainly left matters of warfare to the chief of their tribe. Many young people joined the class because it meant being spared from fighting in battle. Some did this after encouragement from their families, while others came to this resolution on their own. As opposed to fighting and managing battlefields, Druids spent most of their time and energy learning the most they could about philosophy, astronomy, deciphering ancient verse, and the lore of the Gods.

While there is little known about how they conducted their rites in their early days, it's possible they were done in a large clearing under the open air. A location often associated with Druidry is Stonehenge. According to myths, Stonehenge was built by the Druids and used as a temple for their rituals. The structure was built approximately 5000 years ago - long before the first evidence of Druidry. However, since all this is based on oral recollections passed down through many generations, it's unclear whether the Druids were around the time the stones were put in place. The only solid evidence of this theory is that the stones align perfectly with the winter and the summer solstice. This place has a central role in festivities held for the summer solstice - a Sabbat celebrated by many Pagans. The Druids and Celts travel on the longest day of the year every year, even today, to Stonehenge for a small ritual at sunrise. Whether this is a result of the Druids elevating the structure or not, Stonehenge was and still remains a place of spiritual significance for them.

In modern Druidry, it's safe to say that it is somewhat different from its ancient roots - after all, it has been through many changes. Some of the changes were essential for the survival of the practice.

With the arrival of Christianity, Druids were replaced by priests, and their functions were reduced to poets and historians. Yet, they managed to pass down the knowledge throughout centuries of oppression. During the 19th century, the interest in Druidry began to rise again, and new communities were formed in Europe and the United States. Modern Druidry represents a mixture of traditional practices and modern ideas and solutions. For example, animal or human sacrifices are no longer held in their communities. Instead, they offer food, alcohol, and symbolic structures built for this specific purpose, such as a structure stuffed with herbs, candy, etc.

While modern Druids are still required to undergo rigorous training before they are given any responsibilities, they are allowed to learn from books, write down anything they want, and use technology for educational purposes. Retaining the ancient ideology of Druidry, modern Druids are still focused on establishing a reciprocal relationship with their ancestors and between the members of their community. Although their roles are much tamer compared to ancient times, finishing their education grants Druids highly respectable functions in their community.

The Main Druid Philosophy

The central philosophy of Druidry has three equal parts: ancestral veneration, respect for nature, and the belief that everything is infused with nature. The different Druidry associations often have different views on the afterlife. However, almost all believe that the souls move on into another realm or body, continuing a predetermined cycle. They also agree that ancestral spirits hold much wisdom and provide guidance and protection, whether they come back in another form or only convey messages from the otherworld. Nature plays an essential role in each process as it either allows the spirits to visit this world as a living creature or carries the messages through spiritual passageways. Druids often hold rituals for honoring nature's role in their life. Each ritual is built around a particular myth selected by the presiding

Druid. One of their grandest festivities is the welcoming of the spring solstice. They celebrate the awakening of nature's spirit during this festival, bringing them sustenance throughout the year.

Awen

One of the central concepts used in Druidry is Awen - the spirit that provides inspiration. Druids are often required to go on the quest for Awen, pursuing and fulfilling their purpose in life. Whether they become poets, historians, linguists, magicians, priests, or philosophers, is determined by Awen. Finding Awen means understanding where the Druid's strengths lie so that they will follow the path of their destination. Awen is unique to every soul, making it even more challenging to find. When a Druid finds Awen, they gain access to the wisdom of their ancestors in many vital matters. However, each Awen can only be recognized by the person to whom it is linked.

Finding and following their Awen is a sacred rule for the Druids, and it requires paying close attention to their inner spirituality. They must learn to ignore their ego, and everyone and everything else they come into conflict with, and only focus on their intuitive thoughts. This allows them to gain a deeper understanding of themselves, a step that's crucial for finding Awen. Druids are also required to set aside all convictions and prejudice about certain beliefs and their ability to make someone a better person. Since each person has a particular Awen unique to them, the different beliefs also provide a distinctive quality.

Druidry and Celtic Magic

Nothing illustrates better the long-standing relationship between Druidry and Celtic magic than the quest for Awen. The rites, spells, poems, and sacrifices designed to find one's spirituality are all inspired by nature. Celtic magic relies on forging spiritual connections through nature and natural forces. Druids use nature as their muse when enriching their practice and extending their creativity toward finding their life purpose. By spending time in nature and observing its colors, sounds, movements, and overall flow, they become profoundly inspired to create a piece of art, write a poem or a spell, design a ritual or dance, or do whatever they need to uncover the path of Awen. Or they can even create in open air, letting nature permeate their work as the inspiration flows through them.

Nature helps Druids gain a deeper understanding of Awen and how to harvest its benefits. According to Druid teachings, Arwen flows, similar to natural energy. It can travel from one person to another like the wind and touch them like the river touches its bank until it finds its corresponding soul. When this happens, Awen pours into a soul, inspiring its owner to make necessary changes in their life. However, for this to happen, Awen must be allowed to flow freely. The more it flows, the faster it finds the soul it's designed to inspire.

A great way to cultivate the flow of Awen is by reciting the following incantation:

> *"Awen, I sing of you*
>
> *As I call you from the abyss*
>
> *I am ready to receive the Awen that is granted to me*
>
> *I welcome its call*

Even if its power is limited

I know after it will well up

And the inspiration will flow again

You can also use this spell to call upon Awen:

I wish to behold Awen, the source of spiritual inspiration

I wish to find the muse that will guide my voice

So, I can call upon nature and earth

My ancestors and my guides

I ask them to inspire my craft

And let their creativity flow through me

May I receive the blessings of my souls Awen

So, it can stay within me from this day on."

Ritual for Invoking Awen

Another method for invoking Awen is performing a small ritual before any activity requiring higher creativity.

Collect water from a sacred place, like a natural spring or rainwater, and place it on your altar or the place you will perform the ritual. A small amount will be enough, as you can always make more, by adding water from any source. It will remain effective as long as it contains a drop of water from a sacred place. Pour some of the water into a small bowl and start your ritual. Take a few deep breaths, and allow your body and mind to settle. When you feel that your mind has calmed down, close your eyes, and recite the following sentence:

"Let the Awen come to me and inspire me through nature."

Visualize the Awen flowing toward you from the land, sky, and sea, permeating your soul and remaining within you. You seek inspiration when you sense it, open your eyes, and proceed with the endeavor.

Modern Druids

Nowadays, Druids live in smaller groups or are solitary practitioners but often meet with fellow Druids to share their life experiences. They also perform rituals on momentous occasions or celebrate Pagan festivals. Unless the weather makes this impossible, the meetings are held outside, either in someone's garden, a park, or a forest clearing. The people who celebrate together usually belong to one Grove, a group with at least two members who meet from time to time. Grove meetings can be held at times other than during the holidays, depending on the geographical distance that divides the members and people's schedules. For example, initiation of new members or sharing and exploring new teaching can also be an occasion for Druid gatherings. These are typically viewed as social gatherings to strengthen the spiritual connections within the community.

Many Groves are located across the continent, each having a unique way of conducting the teachings and organizing their membership structure. One of the most popular Groves is the UAOD or *United Ancient Order of Druids*. Founded in England, UAOD first spread its teaching through the European continent, later conquering Australia and the United States. This grove is open to all social classes - and in many countries, its purpose is to unite people facing unique challenges. Apart from providing an excellent opportunity for members to improve their knowledge in a specific subject, they often organize charity events to help their community.

Another example of famous Groves is the *Order of Bards, Ovates, and Druids*, known as OBOD. This Grove has a unique hierarchical structure based on the members' years of training and experience. The lowest grade they can occupy is the bardic grade. Once, the Celts' poets made it possible for this belief system to survive by creating various tales about the Celtic culture and the Druids. The second grade is reserved for the Ovates. They taught their community about the benefits of relying on nature in magic and life in general. The highest grade with the highest level of experience is the Druids, versed in journeying and magical practices through which they service the Druid traditions.

The Roles within a Grove

While their lower education level may suggest the Bards occupy a lower rank among the three, it couldn't be further from the truth. Being the custodian of the sacred magic is the greatest honor and influences all three functions of Druidry. These functions are spirituality, education, and politics - all part of a triangle that unites them. It means that while the Bards play an enormous role in education, they are closely connected with the other grades.

Being the masters of divination, the Ovate is responsible for informing their community about all the relevant prophecies and spiritual connections. Additionally, the myths bestow on them the ability to travel in time, allowing them to heal those in need or at least obtain the means to do so. When the Christian Church oppressed Druidry, the Ovate was the only way for the Celts to seek assistance from traditional sources. It taught them how to heal their wounds and persevere in difficult times while carrying on their ancient customs. Although they face different challenges nowadays, Ovate still uses spirituality to heal and guide others. Through spirituality, they even uncover a deeper meaning of life, while ethics guide them towards a path of light.

Druids are often described with the highest ranking, but this is only because of their role; namely, they are responsible for establishing laws or, in modern times, challenging them. Once, they were counseling kings and sovereign on how to achieve peace. Now, their role is reduced to resolving differences within their community and providing legal or financial assistance to those in need, so they need a deeper understanding of the social balance within a community. It's not uncommon for Grove members to train up to 20 years before they gather enough wisdom to occupy this function.

Typically, the purpose of a Grove is to set up a system where all individuals receive the highest education resulting in a class of beings with superior knowledge, allowing them to persevere in life. No matter which grade they specialize in, all members learn Celtic history, genealogy, and the current laws. This allows each grade to rely on the other two with confidence, as together, they can deal with any hurdles much more effectively.

Chapter 5: Ogham, a Magical Alphabet

The Celtic culture is not commonly remembered these days. However, it is a rich and dynamic culture with a long history. Today, the Northern European culture, including the Vikings and other clans that existed in the region, are diluted with the culture of new immigrants and settlers. Moreover, the culture has been exported to several different places across the Western world. It is hard to differentiate from modern Western culture. However, some jewels of the past beautifully preserved have managed to live on. One of the unique elements from the ancient Northern European cultures is the language. Even though it still exists today, it is very different from what it used to be.

The Origins

Ogham, known as the Scared Druidic Alphabet and the Celtic Tree Alphabet, is a language used to write primitive Irish. However, this same alphabet was also used to write several other languages common in the North European region, such as primitive Welsh and Latin. Today, there are few remains of this ancient script other than a few historical artifacts with inscriptions indicating that this language was widely used in much of the Western UK and some regions in Germany.

This language was typically carved onto stones to mark territories and, in some cases, as signs. There is evidence that this language was used in communication, though there aren't many artifacts to back this up. Most experts agree that Ogham is a very old language, probably around in the first century – or even earlier. However, most of the stone artifacts found with Ogham inscriptions are from the 4th century onward. The most recent of these artifacts were dated to the 6th century.

How to Read It

This language is unique from modern languages because the individual alphabet's characters are named after certain objects, a phenomenon known as the Briatharogam tradition. In Ogham, the alphabets are named after different trees, making the language unique and showing the importance of the trees in the culture. The alphabets themselves are known as Feda (trees).

Traditionally, Ogham had 20 alphabets, but five more were added later. The individual alphabets are grouped into 4 "Aicme" (tribes) of five alphabets each. The five alphabets added were Forfeda (special) alphabets but were not commonly used, increasing the number of Aicme to 5, making a total of 25 alphabets.

Similar, but not identical, to some language systems in East Asia, the Ogham alphabet is meant to be written and read vertically, from bottom to top. Nearly every letter other than the exceptional characters is a series of lines drawn through one main vertical line that serves as the "trunk" of the alphabet. All the letters have their unique sound, and some even sound similar to the modern English alphabets. However, pronunciation does vary with the dialect and the language they are being used for. Also, Ogham was commonly used to write names and label things so that people could tell who the object belonged to. Therefore, the structure of the language is not only a name, but rather it is in the third person where the statement sounds like "this belongs to so-and-so" instead of "this is so-and-so's item."

How to Remember It

Traditionally, Ogham was taught in schools alongside modern languages such as English and French. The process was very similar to learning any other language. Students were taught the alphabet through reading, writing, and phonetics and taught how to use these alphabets to construct words. However, since it was never used as a medium of communication, it was only taught to the extent where children could read it and get a good idea of its meaning and how it was constructed.

Suppose you want to memorize the Ogham alphabet and learn the language. In that case, a good starting point is to understand the structure of the letters and put this to your memory. While some sounds might be similar to English alphabets, the text is very different yet simple to remember. You can make things easier by following the alphabet according to the different *Aicme*. All the different Aicme have a specific structure. One Aicme will only have lines jutting out of the trunk to the right, while another will only have them jutting out to the left. In this way, you can simplify the process and remember the alphabets according to Aicme rather than memorizing 25 random characters.

Ogham and the Trees

Ogham has a deep relationship with trees. All the alphabets are named after trees, as previously mentioned. For instance, Beith is named after the Birch tree, and Sail is named after the willow tree. In many illustrations, the tree is part of the alphabet and is meant to make it easier for the readers to associate certain alphabets with the appropriate trees.

The Celtic culture of the past had a very close relationship with trees. Trees were a valuable resource physically and metaphysically for the people of those times. Most importantly, trees are a source of sustenance from the nuts and fruits they produce. They are also home to many birds and animals, which was another way for the Celts to find food quickly, especially during the harsh winter when hunting wasn't always as profitable. Similarly, the wood was used to build structures, make weapons, and, most importantly, make a strong fire to stay warm and cook on.

The significance of trees can also be seen in mythology and folklore, where they play a significant role. Countless Celtic stories are about how metaphysical forces and supernatural beings were related to trees, or the trees had a role in these stories.

Modern Uses of Ogham

The Irish language has gone through many stages of development, and what is considered modern Irish is very different from Ogham in how it is spoken and written. For instance, in modern Irish, the letter "gh," which traditionally had a "g" sound, is no more of a dip in tone than a complete sound. If you were to say Ogham, which technically sounds like Oh-G-Ham, now in modern Irish, it sounds like Om, or Ohm, where the "g" sound is omitted entirely.

There is little functional use for the Ogham language in the modern day. Even the languages it was designed to depict, like Irish and Latin, have very different alphabets. At most, Ogham stands as a memoir of what the Celtic culture used to be. Today, most Ogham is either used in tattoo art or wearable decorations and accessories. The popularity of using Ogham tattoos and other beatifications using the design cues of Ogham is vastly recognized.

Also, due to the relationship of Ogham and divinity, many uses for Ogham words and written depictions are in divinity and magic. Many people still believe in the supernatural power of the Ogham language and practice it according to their beliefs. For others, the Ogham language is the only path to connect with the Celtic gods, and various mantras and chants are used to call upon certain gods from this school of thought. As with many other cultures, there are different gods associated with different things, such as food, protection, and wisdom, and practitioners call upon the different gods depending on their needs and practice.

Ogham in Druid Culture

People in the Celtic culture, like many other cultures, had a caste system, with the Druids being the highest-ranking because they were concerned with metaphysical affairs. The Druids were responsible for all religious matters in the Celtic culture and were also the religious leaders and scholars of the Celtic people. In many cases, the Druids were ranked higher than other state leaders and even kings because they had direct contact with the gods. It was believed that the Druids possessed knowledge, power, and abilities that average humans, including kings and others of high status, lacked.

There were different roles within the Druids category, such as Priests, Shamans, Healers, and Fortune Tellers. In Celtic culture, trees have been the center of many matters similar to Druids. It is believed that the term Druids comes from the Celtic word "Doire," meaning "oak tree." The oak tree symbolizes knowledge and wisdom in Celtic culture and has a very high status among the trees. In the Celtic culture, the trees were usually placed in three categories; The Chieftain Trees, The Peasant Trees, and the Shrub Trees. It is important to note that the different categories of trees didn't make a difference to the tree's hierarchy or status. Instead, it was a way to organize the trees based on their unique characteristics. The oak tree belongs to the Chieftain trees. Examples of Peasant trees include birch, willow, hawthorn, spindle, and honeysuckle. Shrub trees include the apple tree, white poplar, elder, and reed.

Studying the Druids is challenging since so much information is based on information provided by neighboring cultures, such as the

Romans. What makes it more complicated to keep track of is this was not a culture with very clearly defined principles. Unlike other religions, such as Islam's Quran or Christianity's Bible, there was no solid framework in place. There is no defined method of prayer, no weekly or daily prayer process, and no other concept that we can say has stood the test of time. Even though Druidism is still practiced today, it has undergone a series of changes and modifications depending on who and where it is practiced. Interestingly, many regional differences between people who practiced Druidism in the UK, where it was quite cold with long winters, and in Rome, where the temperature was much warmer and longer summers.

Ogham and Divination

Understanding how the Druids worked with divine matters, it is important to note that they used a lunar calendar and not the modern Egyptian solar calendar. This calendar is known as the Celtic Tree Calendar, and it is closely related to the Ogham alphabet. According to this calendar, the year is divided into 13 months, each 28 days long. Similarly, the major holidays are based on the transitions of the weather, and the natural environment is significant in the overall scenario. A new year begins every 31st of October, which is the same day as the last harvest in the United Kingdom. However, this is different for a Druid in the Roman region.

It's also important to note that the Ogham culture and Druidism are based on the concept of *Bnwyfre*, which is similar to the idea of Chi in Eastern philosophy. It relates to the life force we all have within us and how the different religious practices maximize this energy. Also, the culture is based on the Beth-Luis-Nuin concept, that there was first darkness and then light replacing this situation. This also refers to how religion is measured from new moon to new moon.

One of the most important traditions in the Druid culture pertaining to divination is the idea of the Finger Ogham. This is a technique where the hand is used to receive information from higher sources by the Druids. The hand represents the different alphabets of the Ogham alphabet. The consonants are at the tip of the fingers and also represent the lunar months, whereas the vowels are at the base of the fingers. In line with the five fingers, the number five also had a holy status and is usually associated with goddesses and the idea of the changing life cycles. It is also the number that shows the five critical elements of our lives: fire, water, air, earth, and the soul.

Finger Ogham is used as divination. The left hand is held over a person or an object meditated upon. The answer is based on the sensations the person feels in different parts of their hand. The hand is already measured out with letters, vowels, months, and other characteristics, which aids in understanding what the sensations in hand refer to.

Chapter 6: Unlocking Tree Magic

The Celtic culture places much importance on the environment: mountains, rivers, animals, and even plants have a unique place in the culture. However, the most important of all these are the trees. Trees are cherished for multiple reasons and numerous resources, with a spiritual and holy place in the culture. It is reflected in the literature where it praises the trees in many places and highlights how the most affluent people in Celtic cultures had a close affinity with trees.

Importance of Trees in Celtic Culture

For the Celtic people, trees provided several natural resources. Including shelter, building materials, food, protection, and, more importantly, served as the connection between the worlds. We can see that trees have greatly impacted literature, religion, mysticism, and the Celtics' way of life in different ways. Through the surviving Celtic lore, trees have become markers of the ancient cultural heritage of the Celts and allowed their spiritual identity to survive.

Many trees are found in the region where the Celtic people settled, and, for them, all the trees were precious and worthy of respect. The northern UK and bordering European regions are home to some of the thickest forests. Of the many trees within these forests, the Yew tree is given a higher rank than the others. It is seen as the tree that balances everything and brings together the male and female forces in the world.

Trees were so respected because they provided healing. Through the bark of the tree and the oils extracted from it, together with the leaves used as medicine, the Celtic people were able to cure a range of illnesses. Whether it was just a fever or a serious battle wound, there was a tree to provide assistance. Moreover, the Celtics believed that every living thing has a physical and metaphysical side, but they were unique because they extended this belief to plants. Trees were more important in the Celts' culture than in any other, even though general respect and fascination with trees are evident in different cultures of the same period.

Plant Spirit Allies

Many shamanistic approaches in cultures worldwide give plants an exalted status in their ideology. Whether it is things extracted or the physical form of the plant, they are unique creatures with energy and value. In the modern world, medicines derived from plants are chemicals and extracts, whereas, in traditional medicine, especially alternative healing, the plant from which the resource is derived has a value.

In Celtic culture, this concept is encompassed as the plant ally. It is the process where a person identifies with a plant at a much deeper level. They feel the plant's energy, understand what the plant is communicating, and, consequently, better their lives in the process. It is more than being one with nature. It is about internalizing nature and even receiving guidance from the plant ally.

In some cases, the relationship with the plant ally is a momentary interaction. For example, you walk down a path and see a plant reminding you of something or bringing a new thought into your mind. This was the purpose of the plant's interaction. In other cases, the plant ally has a much more permanent position in your life. The plant becomes an entity you can talk to, communicate with, and play a role in your life as with any other human relation. However, plants do not communicate with us as humans do. They are very different beings. The nature of the plant and human is a direct contrast, yet it is still very closely linked. Plants provide in countless physical ways and even more ways spiritually and metaphysically.

Getting a plant spirit ally is not about buying a plant, growing a plant, or even directly interacting with one. Rather, it is about waiting for that moment when a plant genuinely speaks to you. For some, this might be something they discovered in their youth, while many die in search of their plant ally. While there are certain plants you connect with more efficiently, all humans and plants can connect if you are willing to put in the time and effort required.

Tree Meditation

The idea of plant allies is put into motion more effectively when you combine it with a practice such as a tree meditation. Like any other form of meditation, tree meditation can have a range of benefits for both the physical and mental health of the practitioner. The core of tree meditation is aligning the human and plant energy so they are focused and expand as one.

Three main parts of the tree correlate with our existence that we can focus on during tree meditation. The first is the roots. They are buried deep within the soil, far from sight but hugely impact the overall growth and stability of the tree. Moreover, the tree begins its journey underground since the seed is underground and develops first. This relates to the world of dreams and the deep wisdom behind this phenomenon. Even though we don't see dreams with our eyes, we still "see" dreams, and they impact our lives. In the same way, we don't see the roots, but there is no denying they significantly impact the health of the tree.

The second part of the tree is the trunk, and it relates to the material world. As we use the tree trunk for wood to make a range of different things, the visible, physical part of our existence is what we usually do to remain alive – whether working a job you don't really like or tending to physical needs that cannot be avoided. This is the physical part of our existence, which, for some, is the core of their existence, and for others, it is the stepping stone leading them to higher consciousness.

The third part is the branches and the top of the trunk that extends towards the sky. It relates to our consciousness and how we work towards a more elevated level of awareness through meditation. This is where we have access to higher powers, divinity, and energy beyond human capacity.

Like a tree, if we get the right resources, we can continue to grow and develop into strong individuals who are successful in physical and metaphysical aspects, in our personal and professional lives, and ultimately, leading a balanced life.

Important Trees in Celtic culture

Oak

Oak is very close to the Druid people, and even the word Druid comes from the Celtic word for oak, "*Duir.*" Oak has been associated with the most powerful gods in a few different cultures.

The Greeks associated oak with Zeus, the god of gods, and the Celtics associated it with Taranis, the god of thunder. Interestingly, oak trees are associated with the god of thunder, or the god has some control over thunder, and thunderbolts and lightning most commonly hit the oak tree. The strength and longevity of the oak tree have been the subject of discussion for many poets, thinkers, and writers.

Ash

The ash tree also holds a very special place in Celtic culture. It is one of the three sacred trees, the other two being oak and hawthorn. Ash is part of the olive family, although it is much taller and stronger than an olive tree. This tree is not as common today as it was extensively cut down by the Christians in the 7th century when they invaded the Celtic region, and this practice symbolized their victory. According to tradition, St. Patrick used a wand made from ash to protect against snakes, and even today, the preferred material for a magic wand is ash. It is also believed that this wood has power over water, and when Irish immigrants were moving to America, they often carried a bit of ash wood to protect themselves from drowning.

Apple

The apple tree is commonly found in fairy tales in Celtic culture. There are countless accounts of a magical maiden with access to another realm using the apple as bait. In many stories, this apple also had superpowers. It either provided privileges like never-ending youth or regenerated as soon as it was consumed. In nearly all cases, this maiden used the apple to lure a handsome man to the other side of existence, possibly to a parallel universe. Apples were a fruit that not only gave good health, but which also gave life and were associated with rebirth, and why apples were often buried with people to give them fuel in the next life and to assist them with their rebirth. Interestingly, slices of apples were found in graves in Africa and other parts of Europe. These tombs and graves date as far back as 5000 BC, and, in some cases, there are graves from 7000 BC with traces of apples. We can assume those people used apples similarly or, at least, apples had some value for those passed on to the next life. However, Ireland is home to a unique species of apple known as the crab apple. The traditional apple was most likely brought to the region by the Romans as it does not naturally occur in the region.

Elder

The elder is also an important tree, and while it isn't part of the sacred trees, it does share similar status. Similar to rules concerning the hawthorn tree, it was forbidden to cut down an elder tree. The elder tree was used for many different purposes in the culinary, mystical, and medical departments since the flowers and the berries can be used to make wine. However, the wine made from the flowers was used as a celebratory drink, whereas the wine made from the fruit was used for divinations as it induced hallucinations. The elder tree was challenging to deal with. For instance, if the wine-making process isn't done properly, it could be fatal. Everything from the seeds, leaves, the bark, the flowers, and even the fruit can be poisonous if not harvested at the right time.

The culture of not cutting down the elder tree is common to other parts of Europe, and while the reasoning differs, not permitted to cut this tree remains the same. Later, the elder tree got a bad rep due to the Christians of that time, as they believed the cross on which Christ was crucified was made from elder wood. Similarly, Judas, who betrayed Jesus, is thought to have hung himself from the elder tree, so it was inherently an omen of bad luck. This is most likely where stories of the elder witches came from, as it was a tree associated with the devil.

Alder

Growing along streams, rivers, and swamps, the alder is linked to mysterious forces, secrecy, and bad fortune. Being a historically engrained cultural and spiritual orientation all these years, people in certain Irish communities still believe that running into an alder tree is a sign of bad luck or misfortune. The gloomy atmosphere of the alder woods makes them the ideal hiding place for fairies and other spirits – good or bad. The green flowers and leaves of the alder are perfect for concealing supernatural beings from human eyes. To walk amongst them would mean to disturb their lives. Therefore, these woods were seldom visited, particularly around the spring when fairies are said to be the most active.

However, since alder grows in wet conditions, the older trunks become very hard. The Celts made use of this quality by drying out mature trees and using them as charcoal to light fires with intense heat, like those needed to forge their weapons. As the alder tree burned under the heated-up metal, it also imbued the weapons with natural spiritual power.

A living and healthy alder tree is usually pale in color; you can find out that it has been cut or affected one way or another if a deeper, warmer color starts spreading across it; almost as if it's bleeding. This picture gave another reason for the Celts to develop a series of negative associations with this tree, linking it to death, injuries, and ailments. At the same time, they revered alder and even linked its roots to fertility. The same way alder roots found their way to thrive in wet soil; they can be used in rituals for enhancing the fertility of the land and one's own life.

Yew

While most sources tie the yew to Roman mythology, their records show that this tree has been revered long before its dominion over Europe. Native to the British Isles, the yew tree has been part of Druidic practices ever since the Celts arrived there. They observed that fallen branches of the tree could take roots and form new trees, revealing the yew's incredible regenerative abilities. Due to this, the yew becomes the symbol of death and resurrection. The dead were buried with yew tree branches to help their souls move on, a practice that continued well into the Christian era. A similar symbol of cultural resistance was planting yew trees besides churches and using branches during Christian ceremonies.

Another connection between the sacred yew tree and death was its toxicity. Druidic teachings indicate that even slips of yew needles were enough to cause an illness or even death. However, a tincture made from the flesh of yew berries can cure ailments, especially those caused by an inflammation of some sort. The yew's power is the strongest if harvested during the new moon.

Hazel

The Druids revered the hazel tree for its ability to grant higher wisdom; "*cno*," derived from "*cnocach*," meaning wisdom, is the Gaelic word for hazelnut. According to ancient Celtic lore, nine hazel trees grew around a sacred body of water in which salmon grew. When matured, the nuts fell into the water and were eaten by the fish. The salmon absorbed all the wisdom the nuts contained and were a suitable vessel for its distribution amongst humans, becoming the Salmon of Knowledge. If a Druid wanted to expand his knowledge, he needed to catch salmon with bright spots on its body. The brighter spots the fish had, the more hazelnuts it consumed - and the more wisdom they received.

According to Celtic mythology, hazel is also associated with other magical springs and wells, not only the one containing the Salmon of Knowledge. Mature hazelwood contained just as much wisdom as the nuts did. Wands made from this wood could settle arguments or, in some cases, even administer the law. Whichever part of hazel was used, it was fundamental to preserve the tree's ability to survive and regenerate.

Due to all this, cutting down an entire hazel tree often carried the death sentence as punishment.

Parts of a hazel tree were also used for Druidic rituals as an offering, fire, or containers for other tools. Forked twigs of hazel were used for divination – as it was known to help locate bodies of water and other natural sources of magic. The Celts also believed that young hazel leaves have healing abilities for humans and animals. They would make tea out of it to aid digestion and feed the leaves to cattle to improve milk yield.

Willow

Since most willow species thrive close to waters, there is little wonder Celtic folklore is full of tales based on this watery theme. The moon is also often associated with both the willow tree and the water. When covering the trunk, the water empowers the willow with spiritual magic, and the cycle of the moon affects how much of the tree will be covered. It's believed that willow contains less power during the waning phase of the moon. Therefore, if one wants to take advantage of the willow's benefits, they should wait until the waxing phase to harvest.

Willow has found many uses in Celtic healing rituals and practices. When made into a bitter infusion, willow bark alleviates fevers, pain, and inflammation. Deities associated with the power of the moon are often offered willow parts as an expression of gratitude, reverence, or need for assistance. Being a hunter-gatherer nation, the Celts have also used willow for building boats, coracles, houses, and much more.

Apart from the Celtic lore, the power of the willow is also illustrated in Greek mythology. Their priestesses and healers used this sacred tree for water magic, healing, and other witchcraft practices. The Greeks also linked willow to wisdom and inspiration, and the tree was revered by poets and philosophers alike.

Holly

Nowadays, holly berries and leaves are linked with Christmas, a Christian religious holiday. This symbolism stems from the similarities between the spiny leaves of the tree and Jesus' crown of thorns and between the red berries and savior's drops of blood he shed for humanity. Historical artifacts show that holly was part of similar pre-Christian Yule celebrations. The Celts would bring Holly berries and leaves into their homes to brighten up the cold and dark winter days. Young men would adorn themselves with holly leaves, while girls would wear ivy and walk around in their community. This ritual is said to cause winter to end soon and the New Year's fertility to re-emerge.

The use of holly around Yuletide emanates from the tales of Celtic mythology. According to these, the Oak King ruled over half the year from the winter to the summer solstice. Then, he battled with the Holly King, who, defeating him, took over to rule the other half of the year. His rule lasted until the winter solstice came again, and another battle between the kings ensued – and this time, it ended up with the Oak King`s victory.

The stories depict the Holly King as a giant wielding a holly bush and covered in holly. A similar illustration is found in the Arthurian legend - where the Green Knight arrived wearing a similar ensemble challenging Gawain during Christmas celebrations.

Apart from adding color and a piece of nature to their home, the Celts brought holly into their homes for several other reasons. They used the leaves as a source of winter fodder for livestock because they believed the magical properties of holly would protect the animals. Planting holly near houses was another common practice used to ward off malicious spirits and bad intentions. The fall of the entire tree was believed to be the work of these spirits and was considered bad luck. However, if only parts of the tree had fallen to the ground, they had already fulfilled their protective function outside the home and were safe to bring inside.

At other times, holly branches with leaves served as shelters for benevolent faeries inside the home. The leaves allowed these beings to hide from the harsh winter as well as from the people living in the home. Another Celtic tale depicts how holly was used to decide who had the most say in the household. Holly leaves come in two forms; prickly and smooth. Whichever type was brought into the home first around Yuletide determined whether the husband or the wife would rule their household through the following year.

Hawthorn

This tree is commonly associated with fairies and is often thought to be a gentle tree with magical powers. Out of respect, it is often referred to as the lone bush or simply the thorn as it is considered bad manners to mention fairies by their names. If one tree could be even worse to cut down than the elder tree, it would have to be the lone bush. It is considered a bad luck omen if one even hurts the hawthorn tree. It is so highly esteemed that many people won't even talk about it, let alone damage one due to respect and fear. However, Hawthorn trees have always been considered a source of protection from threats not visible to the human eye. Evil spirits, witches, and other threats are thought to be powerless in front of the majestic hawthorn tree.

Interestingly, in modern Britain, the hawthorn tree is considered a sign of love and prosperity. In the summertime, lovers would frequently meet under the loving shade of a hawthorn tree. Across the border, in Greece, brides often wore a decorative hawthorn crown. Even the wedding torch was made from hawthorn tree branches, and it was good luck for the couple exchanging vows.

On the contrary, Christians (not in the modern-day) believed the crown of thorns placed on Jesus Christ's head during the crucifixion was made from the hawthorn tree. Naturally, this school of thought would not favor this tree quite as much.

Many of the beliefs associated with the different trees of the regions have managed to live on. Even today, we see many people, even those not from Celtic culture, abide by these ideologies and respect the trees as the Celtic people did. While trees may not play such an essential role in our lives today, they are still crucial, especially for the Druids.

Chapter 7: Practicing Ogham Divination

The Ogham text is used for divination by Celtics and those wanting to participate in the Ogham culture for the divinity aspect. Similar to tarot cards used by fortune tellers and other systems used by palmists, the Ogham alphabet is used to decipher information about the past, present, and future. The Ogham culture gives insight into any situations you might face. Many people use the Ogham divination system daily to understand how they should pursue their day, what challenges they might face, and how they should deal with these matters. The other thing that makes this form of divination quite interesting and unique is that different people can interpret various things differently. The meaning can be adjusted to suit your personal preferences. This is an important aspect that requires time to perfect. This doesn't mean that you will read what you want to read or that would kill the purpose of divination. Instead, it means that the meanings you assign to different characters may be different.

For instance, if a certain character means something positive, this may indicate something good is coming your way. But, for someone else, this may mean a day when they won't have to make stressful decisions, or they can take things a little easier. So, the way you interpret the signs may be different, and that is fine. Many people who practice divination through the Ogham letter find that the meanings they associate with the letters change over time. Since all the alphabets are named after trees, or at least associated with a tree, they all have different characteristics reminiscent of the nature or structure of the tree they represent. For instance, the olive tree is generally seen as a feminine tree. It gives plenty of nutritious fruit, has healing properties, is small compared to an oak or mahogany tree, and is rather slow growing.

When one person looks at these factors, they may think they will have a fruitful day, a day where things will be warm and happy as the olive tree prospers in warmer weather, or find something that yields multiple benefits or expect a small positive surprise like the olive tree. On the other hand, a different person may interpret this as a challenging day since it takes a while to develop, or a day when they have to be careful about the environment as the olive tree requires consistent weather to fruit properly. They may be considering multiple risks since the olive tree gives multiple things, but even if one thing goes wrong, multiple things could be lost or wasted.

So, it depends on how you look at things, your situation, your walk of life, and other factors. Again, the more you learn about the alphabet, the more you will know and the better your understanding can be drawn from this divination. Let's look at the two ways Ogham divination is practiced.

Ogham Divination through Staves or Tiles

The process for divination through these tools is relatively straightforward and can be modified to meet your requirements. Generally, it is suggested that you use at least three staves or three tiles to uncover the message. However, in some cases, where the question is a simple yes or no, it is suitable only to draw a single stave or tile. In other situations, and depending on your needs where you seek a more in-depth answer to a more open-ended question, it may be appropriate to use more staves or tiles.

When performing the actual divination, there are a few ways to do it. Some people prefer to allocate a certain time of day to practice divination, which is somewhat of a ritual. Unlike tarot cards, where the expert merely reads the cards whenever you visit, when doing your divination, there are different ways you can choose to do it. Some people prefer to say a prayer, light candles, or even cleanse themselves before they do the reading. For others, it is something they do casually, whenever they feel the need. Also, some people prefer practicing in a particular part of the home, or outdoors or doing it during the day or at night. Once you start, you may feel better doing it before going to bed to help you through the next day or prefer to do it first thing in the morning.

These are variables you can work on according to what suits your needs, and they will get more refined as you practice.

When using the Ogham alphabets for divination, you only need to use the main 20 characters as the exceptional characters will not yield much value. Also, it is helpful to compile a list of traits and features of the various alphabets and learn the history of each. The more you know about each character the stave, or the title expresses, the more intricate and accurate your deductions.

For instance, the oak tree, known as Duir in Ogham, is represented by a vertical line with two perpendicular lines pointing outwards to the left. Duir is the name of the alphabet, and as a word, it means door. In this way, this tree is seen as the doorway to higher consciousness and the unseen world. Similarly, the oak tree is considered the king of the forest, or the king of the trees in the forest, a slow-growing tree that develops a strong and large structure with deep roots and a broad and tall network of branches. The oak tree is a very resilient plant and can withstand very long cold winters.

The wood is known for its quality. It is extremely smooth and hard, and the grain goes in the same direction. This wood doesn't deform very easily and can withstand various harsh conditions if processed correctly. Due to the toughness of this wood, it is not common for termites or other insects to cause harm, and it is very durable. Even though the original color is light, thanks to the natural patterns, just a bit of varnish or light tan can really make the wood stand out. Just looking at the tree, you can see its presence demands respect, and it oozes strength in every way. It is a majestic tree associated with wisdom, strength, patience, and resilience. It also represents justice, equality, prosperity, health, and protection.

Also, the Duir is a calendar star, and it governs people born between June 10th and July 17th. It is also associated with the number 7. The associated color is gold, the main feature is strength, the associated animal is a white horse, and associated plants include the mistletoe and the coltsfoot.

If you find Duir in your divination, know that you must handle the matter with courage and strength to walk through the door of change. You also need to maintain integrity and think things through as the wise oak tree takes time to grow and expands in every direction. Consider all the possibilities, and whatever you decide, be prepared to hold this stance for the long term. The oak tree yields acorns that are also very dense and solid protection for the seed within them. In the same way, when you see Duir in your divination, know that you have to act with wisdom, or the wisdom is already within you, and you must have the courage to act on it. Within these steps you are about to take, there is wisdom and a precious result, one that may yield a very strong outcome like the little oak seed that yields a mighty tree. It's essential to remember that the Duir is the doorway to experience, knowledge, information, and an overall up-gradation of consciousness. Even though the decisions are challenging, they are the way to go.

In this way, the Ogham alphabets can be interpreted in different styles, and the deeper your understanding of the alphabet, the more information you will draw from the stave or tile.

How to Create Ogham Staves

Some people prefer to make the wooden staves out of the wood they are associated with. So, the Duir stave would be made out of oak. However, others argue that they should all be made out of the same wood so that you can't tell the difference when picking them out. Similarly, some prefer to have staves of a smaller size, small enough to fit them all in your hand. Others like to have rather large staves, a foot long and a few inches thick. If you want something portable, stick to a smaller size, but you can make them larger if it's a home kit.

The process is quite simple. You have to inscribe into the stave the different alphabets. Some people prefer to burn the alphabet into the stave, some prefer to scratch it in, while others merely stain it into the wood. It all depends on what you have and what you are comfortable doing.

Also, you can finish and polish the wood as you prefer or leave it plain and raw.

How to Create Ogham Tiles

You can create the tile from clay, wood, ceramic, or any material you like. Some people even make small tiles the size of dominoes made out of marble or a different stone and made with a nice finish in a color of their choice. Usually, the tiles are made in a rectangular shape, although you can use squares, hexagons, or triangles. It's all a matter of preference and what is viable for you. The alphabet must only be written on one side of the tile as the orientation can change the alphabet entirely. Also, consider the material depending on how you want to use the tiles. Some people prefer to pick up a few tiles and throw them onto the floor, while others like to pick each one individually and place it gently in front of them. It is recommended that the staves and tiles be made from natural materials rather than man-made materials, so they are more connected with the earth, and this helps to keep their energy as pure as possible.

Also, when creating tiles or staves, it is important to mark the tiles from the first and third families of alphabets as they look the same, the only difference being the direction in which the lines are pointed. If you see the same tile inverted, it can cause confusion. Similarly, even the tile with diagonal lines has an orientation, so it's good to make a small mark on the stave or the tile to ensure you have placed it down in the correct orientation and you are reading correctly. Usually, these tiles will not require washing, but some people prefer to wash their tiles and staves to cleanse the energy and recharge for the next use.

If you prefer, say a prayer before your question or simply move directly into your question and pull out the alphabets to see the responses. Saying the question out loud or in your mind is fine either way. However, be thoughtful about the question. Make it as concise and accurate as possible so that you don't have to ask too many follow-up questions and get the most out of each question. At the end of the divination, it is considered good etiquette to say a word of thanks to the forces that helped you find your answer and treat your alphabets with respect. If you prefer, you can sit outside under a tree or on the ground to get your energy better connected to the Earth's energy.

Chapter 8: Conducting Celtic Rituals

Ceremonies and rituals are practices dating back to the first recorded human history. For example, Paleolithic cave paintings dating back more than 10,000 years suggest that our ancestors gathered around fires performing fertility dances. They also partook in other spiritual ceremonies that celebrated their hunts. Regardless of religion, ethnicity, geographic location, or culture, all societal groups in humanity have distinctive rituals, traditions, and ceremonies that give meaning and purpose.

Unfortunately, we no longer hold rituals and ceremonies of the same significance and importance as we once did. In this age, we use science and evidence to lead our lives. Rituals and ceremonies have become widely frowned upon due to their lack of functionality and scientific corroboration. They are now typically exclusive to native tribes or peoples and religious institutions.

While we don't need ceremonies, traditions, and rituals in today's digitally-driven world, many people don't realize they are an intrinsic part of humanity, a human instinct, even. Our ancestors needed the power of rituals because they gave them a sense of structure. They helped them make sense of a world they truly understood as they prayed for rewarding hunts, stable weather, and fertility. Today, we can check the weather predictions a week ahead and not worry about harvesting or hunting for food. Although we now have more access to life's riches and a deeper understanding of the world around us, the magic of life is no longer imminent.

The diminishing role of rituals has deprived us of a very important aspect of life. Not only are our rituals important for our happiness, but they also allow us to maintain and build communities, essential for a healthy society.

Food, water, clothing, shelter, air, sleep, love, hygiene, and communication are important for human survival, and we also need rituals and ceremonies. Rituals help instill an inner sense of belonging. They remind us that life and our human experience are a lot greater than we can ever comprehend. They reach beyond our physical existence. Ceremonies and rituals help us develop a deeper appreciation for the universe and enrich our perception of archetypes like continuity, faith, devotion, and unity. Rituals help us build a connection to the divine and serve as a pathway to recounting the capacity of existence, which is rather baffling to the human mind.

This is why rituals are vital to finding success and thriving in life. They donate a sense of direction in our physical experience. They allow us to forge deeper connections with ourselves and our souls and the higher power that grants life. Connecting with people interested in Celtic magic is awesome. However, conducting ceremonies and partaking in rituals establishes a sense of unity rather than separation. Even if they don't necessarily live in your area, sharing your experiences online, through Facebook groups, blogs, or forums shows that others strive and long for the same things as you.

While modern science undoubtedly allows us to comprehend the numerous mysteries of life, the need for belonging, especially regarding something we feel so deeply for, still persists. We need rituals and ceremonies in times of great uncertainty the most. They help us stay grounded through transformative experiences and big changes in life, such as marriage or death.

Even though some rituals, like funerals, birthdays, and weddings, are still present and celebrated, many others have been abandoned. Perhaps it is because many traditional rituals are too complicated to fit into our modern-day lives. The rituals don't cater to our deepest needs and yearning for meaning. Sadly, the lack of important rituals in our lives disconnects us from ourselves, our culture, or our beliefs. Therefore, it's important to incorporate them into the fast-paced life and ever-changing nature of the world we live in.

Choosing rituals or even making your own can be challenging, especially if you don't follow a certain belief or show an interest in a solid spiritual endeavor. If you're reading this book, you're likely to be interested in Celtic magic and traditions. Fortunately, this chapter includes various simple Celtic rituals you can try. It also explains the five Celtic rituals and how they were conducted in ancient times. You will learn how to conduct a modern Celtic ritual and its Druid, Scottish, and Irish variations.

Ancient Rituals

The Celts held rituals when the community was subject to great stress. They also conducted rituals for specific purposes and followed certain situations. Scholars also believed that the Celts followed a certain astronomy-based schedule, particularly a schedule based upon the phases of the moon. They offered incantations and prayed to their gods. They also made votive offerings to gain the favor of the gods. They believed that this would help them get outcomes in their favor and ward off disasters like famine, floods, drought, or wars. These offerings typically took the form of jewelry, bejeweled armors and weapons seized from the enemies, pottery vessels, and other precious goods. They also offered foodstuffs, and, in case someone had recovered from an illness, they'd offer the affected body part.

The Celts were very concerned with rituals as they helped bring structure and order to their lives and keep up with changing seasons and the passage of time. Rituals also allowed them to make sense of and find meaning in the world around them. They used rituals and celebrations to understand and explain happenings they couldn't control. For instance, they used the Wheel of the Year, which split the year into eight portions, and celebratory feasts, to mark the change of seasons and comprehend the changes in land fertility, hunts, etc. The way they attempted to understand natural phenomena and happenings shows how they tried to go beyond the material world and forge connections with the forces they believed affected the dynamics of life. There are five main Celtic rituals; magic rituals, curative rituals, divination rituals, transmigration rituals, and rituals performed at seasonal feasts.

1. Magic Rituals

As you can infer from their name, Magic rituals involved the use and concept of magic. The "Magic of the Head" was one of the most significant magic rituals. It revolved around the belief that the human mind, or head, is vital to magical practices. They also believed that it was of great potency and power, which is why the Celts often beheaded their enemies at war so they could preserve and put them on display.

- **Human Sacrifices**

    Magic rituals involved curative plants (more on that later), and they are portrayed in various Druid tales. Evidence of calling onto a god to invoke blessings and curses is apparent on lead plates and other artifacts. Human sacrifice was also an aspect of magic rituals. There is evidence of a man from Lindow moss in England who was ritualistically hit on the head, strangled, and drowned. Other stories suggest that Celtic people often practiced the ritualistic killing of humans. Various Druid spells are linked to Druid priests and women, claiming they could control or influence natural elements. Many tales included claims of invisibility and the ability to turn rocks into armies of armed men and move mountains.

- **Wands**

    Wands also played a great role in Druid magic rituals. Druids believed that wands were living objects, metaphysically speaking, because they believed trees have dryads or special spirits or souls. The significance of dryads (the human spirit in its essential nature) is that they're divisible. They're considered a quality of wood, like color, texture, luster, grain, and other properties. Therefore, the dryad is distributed throughout the entire tree or log. So, when the pieces are used to make wands, they still contain a whole dryad, like the entire tree. While using or making wands, Druids often employed rituals and recited blessings to activate and awaken the wand's dryad. Wands were considered more than just tools. They were also a practitioner's magical partner.

- **Smudging**

    Smudging was also another aspect of the Druid magical practices. Smudging involved the burning of a stick or bundle of dried herbs. The purpose of this practice was to clear away negative energy and create positive vibes. A smudge stick differs from incense because it's made of plenty of leaves and has to be waved or moved around so that the smoke spreads effectively. On the other hand, incense is mixed with essential oils and is often transformed into granules, cones, or attached to sticks, and you don't need to wave it around.

Druids paid extra attention to the types of herbs that they gathered and used for smudging. They also typically made, and still make, their smudge sticks because each herb has its own characteristics and traditional uses. Your choice, along with your intentions, determines what your smudging practice attracts into your life. For instance, you can use the same herb to get rid of negative energy and attract good fortune and love into your life. Look up the characteristics of various herbs to know their purposes.

2. Curative Rituals

Curative rituals are associated with restoration and healing. The Celts believed there were ten elemental constructs for healing: water, stones, herbs, fire, nature, music, deities, symbols, rituals, and storytelling. Each element connected to or supported another element, acting as a dimension of Celtic daily life.

• Alternative Healing

In essence, Druid healing practices promote the support of spiritual and physical health through energy manipulation, exercise, and balanced or healthy diets. Although Druidry is a long-established spiritual tradition, Druids are always encouraged to experiment with their preferences and beliefs regarding magic, deities, and other spiritual endeavors. This is particularly important because there is no solid method for conductive rituals. Ancient and modern-day Druids typically incorporate alternative healing methods, such as healing rituals and spells, herbs, and Reiki, into their personal practices.

Druid healing practices involve the use of healing herbs the Celts traditionally used. Some herbs like vervain and St.

John's Wort are used to make tinctures and teas, while others are used for their symbolic meanings. Plants were also popularly used by the Irish for their healing properties.

Many individuals accompanied the use of plants with spells and charms. It was believed that bladder stones could be cured with wild garlic infusions, epilepsy with juniper berries juice, and intestinal worms with tansy infusions. Sores and cuts were also widely healed using figwort. There is evidence of hemlock removing cancer growth with the right invocation.

- **Animals and Their Products**

It was believed that passing an individual under a horse's belly would cure their cough. The Celts believed that the horse had to be white, while many areas around the British Isles believed the horse needed to be piebald. Of course, where you lived as a Celt came with a few unique rituals. The Irish Celts, for example, believed that dandelion potion could cure asthma. The Scottish Celts, on the other hand, believed asthma could be cured if you smeared deer grease on the soles of your feet.

- **Spells and Charms**

In Celtic customs, fairies have always been known to be especially dangerous during childbirth. To save a mother and protect her child from being abducted, a piece of iron was usually placed in the mother's bed. The infant also had to be baptized as soon as possible to be kept safe from the evil spirits. Charms were also routinely used to protect people from injuries, especially those caused by the evil eye or obtained during battle.

Druid healing rituals and spells are often a combination of invocation and serve as a healing plea. They also visualize healing light or energy delivered to the suffering individuals. Many also use healing herbs to enhance the effect of the spell. They may also indulge in meditations that help rid undesirable energy and reduce stress levels.

- **Water**

  It's known that the source of all life is water, and with that in mind, it comes as no surprise that it was used in many rituals. Add to that, if the water came from a specific well or river, it was thought to have incredible medicinal powers. The Irish believed that ailments such as mumps could be cured if the suffering individual drank water from specific rivers three times. Certain wells were also thought to reduce toothaches. They were also associated with local gods, and so, their healing characteristics were linked to the deities.

3. Divination Rituals

Apart from being associated with fortune-telling, divination also involves revealing hidden inner or external dynamics. It can also be defined as a very deep self-understanding and knowledge and the ability to know the unapparent reasons behind happenings.

Druids used numerous methods of divination, encompassing simple methods, such as weather-witching, to more complex ones like the observation of bird flight. They also examined animal behavior and elucidated planetary configurations. The Irish Druids used cloud divination or Neldoracht and a more sophisticated method, Tarbhfeis, which required the individual to wrap themselves up in a bull's hide. It was believed that the clairvoyant person could refine their abilities by doing so.

You can enhance your clairvoyant abilities by indulging in a wide array of divination rituals better suited for modern-day life. For example, you can work with sacred animals and traditional Druid and Celtic plants and herbs.

4. Transmigration Rituals

Transmigration is also known as reincarnation. In a spiritual, religious, philosophical sense, transmigration is the concept that a person's soul or spirit starts a new life in a different body or physical form following their physical death.

The Celts believed in life after death. Therefore, they buried individuals with their ornaments, weapons, and food. The Druids taught the principle of the transmigration of souls. They also explained the significance of nature and the power of the gods. The Celts practiced urnfield burial, which involved creating the body and placing its ashes in an urn. However, this only lasted until the 6th to the 8th century BCE, when they started practicing Inhumation burial rites (full-body burials). However, the process differed according to a person's class. Slaves and lower-class individuals were buried in normal graves, with a few prized possessions, while the nobles were buried with swords, jewelry, wine flagons, chariots, and more. They usually scattered large rocks and mounds around the burial site to ward off evil spirits.

The Irish believed in the existence of an otherworld. The otherworld was thought to be an island in the vast seas or located underground. They explained it as a country free of death, illness, and aging. They thought it was a happy place where a day was equivalent to a hundred Earth years.

5. Rituals at Seasonal Feasts

As we mentioned above, feasts were a significant aspect of the Celtic culture. They had season feasts to celebrate important changes and dates in their calendars. They used a Wheel of the Year to split the year into eight portions to mark the cyclical alternation of seasons. They mainly celebrated four fire festivals every year; Samhain, Imbolc, Bealtaine, and Lughnasadh. Equinoxes and solstices are also integrated into the wheel, with these four main festivals. The so-called quarter-festivals are Yule, Ostara, Litha, and Mabon. Each celebration accompanied a set of unique rituals, discussed in more depth in the following chapter.

Rituals are a vital aspect of humanity. They help keep us reminded of purpose and donate a sense of structure and were conducted in every culture throughout history, and played a vital role in Celtic, Druid, Irish, and Scottish traditions. The most significant traditions were magic, curative, divination, transmigration, and seasonal feast rituals. There are numerous modern-day-friendly ways you can incorporate these practices into your personal routine.

Chapter 9: Sacred Celtic Holidays

Celtic holidays hold a special place in ancient and modern pagan rituals and can significantly affect druidic magic and Celtic rituals. Each holiday is associated with a seasonal event and falls between solar events and turning points of the year. Although ancient, these holidays are still celebrated throughout the Celtic culture, with many traditional rituals carried out specifically on these holidays.

When learning about Celtic rituals and spells, it's important to understand the significance of these sacred holidays to best channel their energy through spells and rituals. While the ancient Celts had specific rituals for each holiday, their importance in modern paganism cannot be understated. Therefore, it's best that you understand the sacred Celtic holidays and their energies before carrying out special rituals on these holidays.

Listed below, in chronological order, are the eight most important sacred Celtic holidays throughout the year, starting with St Brigid's day in February through to the winter solstice in December.

1. St Brigid's Day - Imbolc

The year's first Celtic holiday, St Brigid's day, marks the first day of spring and is celebrated on February 1st. This day is associated with Ireland's first native saint, St Brigid, the Abbess of one of the first convents in Ireland. The symbolic representation of this day is associated with a straw or a red cross. Brigid day is associated with poetry, healing, and fertility and marks the beginning of a new season of hope.

Historic Celtic Rituals

According to ancient Celtic tradition, St. Brigid's day marked the beginning of the year. It was, therefore, celebrated with great fervor to secure St. Brigid's protection and promise of great abundance for life ahead. Ancient Celtic rituals during St. Brigid's day included the following:

- Ancient Celts celebrated Imbolc as one of the quarter days that marked a transition from one season to the next. The festivities took place on the eve of the day because this time was considered effective for spells and rituals.

- The traditional festive meal of St Brigid's day included a supper of potatoes with freshly churned butter, followed by apple cakes or barmbrack and tea.

- St Brigid's crosses held a special place in tradition. Many people believed that St Brigid would pass by and bless the homes with these crosses hung in her honor on the day of the festivities. There were many regional variations in the making and hanging of these crosses, but most served the same purpose to attract the saint's blessings.

- Leftover material from the crosses and old crosses from the previous year was sprinkled on the land to protect crops and livestock or incorporated into the animals' bedding.

- The tradition of a Brat Bríde or Ribín Bríde was common in ancient Celtic traditions. People would leave a piece of clothing or ribbon on the windowsill, which was endowed with healing or curative properties by St. Brigid on the eve of her feast.

- Many wells were dedicated to St. Brigid and visited by people on the eve of St Brigid's day every year.

Modern Celebrations

Modern paganism celebrates Brigid's day in various ways. While some modern pagans follow most ancient Celtic rituals, others have defined newer ways to celebrate this feastful day. Some modern pagan celebrations include:

- Special Imbolc feasts with traditional meals like dumplings, baked bread, eggs, milk, colcannon, etc., are dedicated to the saint Brigid.

- A cleansing bath ritual is customary to wash away the negative energy from the dark season (winters) in preparation for the new season.

- Brigid crosses are made through various methods, styles, and materials and hung outside homes to attract blessings and positive energy.

- A fire lighting ritual is followed to beckon the warmth of the coming sun. Whether you light a bonfire, fireplace, or even a candle depends on you.

Self-Purification Ritual

A self-purification ritual on Brigid's day is perfect for harnessing the purifying energies that St Brigid brings. As the mistress of fire, the saint has immense power over this element's cleansing and purifying capabilities. Use this simple ritual to cleanse away all the darkness and debris from the winter.

- For this rite, you will require a candle, incense, a bowl of water, and some salt.

- Find a quiet place to sit and center yourself by taking in a few deep breaths.

- Invite St Brigid into your ritual space and feel her presence.

- Light the candle to represent fire, and ask Brigid to purify your life.

- Next, sprinkle some salt on your skin, representing the earth, and ask Brigid to cleanse your body.

- Light the incense to represent air, and ask Brigid to clear your mind.

- Finally, take the bowl of water and sprinkle it on and around your body to purify your emotions.

2. St. Patrick's Day - Spring Equinox

One of Ireland's and the Celtic traditions' biggest holidays, St. Patrick's Day, or the spring equinox, is celebrated on March 17th as a tribute to the patron saint of Ireland. The time of spring equinox has certain significance in Celtic tradition because the Celts determined seasons using natural time. Hence, the solstice and equinox events hold tremendous importance, especially for certain rituals and spell work to be effective. As the name suggests, spring equinox is a time of perfect balance, where the day and night are almost entirely of equal length and considered a sacred time by Celtic ancestors.

Historic Celtic Rituals

While the spring equinox holds greater importance compared with St Patrick's Day in Celtic tradition, both are celebrated with equal fervor annually. Historically, the spring equinox has held great importance for Celtic rituals and spell-work as it represents the perfect balance between day and night, and many spells work best during this time. In Celtic tradition, the spring equinox was celebrated as Ostara, where rebirth and renewed life were celebrated. Historical rituals included:

- Initially, Easter originated from Ostara, where ancient Celtic people decorated eggs.

- New fires were lit as a symbol of new beginnings and rebirth.

- Ancient feast celebrations included meals that honored the coming of spring, including eggs, shoots and sprouts, and other early spring greens.

Modern Celebrations

Modern pagans all over the world celebrate the spring equinox or Ostara and practice specific magic and spell-work during this time. Here are some of the celebrations and rituals carried out during the spring equinox.

- The Ostara altar is set up using balancing symbols to represent the spring equinox.

- Many pagans practice earth meditation to ground themselves to reconnect with the earth and nature.

- Magic related to rebirth and growth is practiced during the spring equinox. This could include egg magic, serpent magic, flower magic, and magical gardening.

Rebirthing Ritual

As spring symbolizes the completion of the rebirth cycle, many pagans use the spring equinox to complete a rebirthing ritual to balance their energy and find harmony within themselves. The following steps should be followed.

- You will need to use your Ostara altar with a black sheet, a bowl of soil, water, candles, and incense.

- Wear the black sheet or ritual robe, and draw a circle around your Ostara altar.

- Enter this circle, kneel, and recite the Ostara ritual verses.

- One by one, move the items around your body to represent each element.

- Start with the salt, then the candles, the incense, and lastly, some water.

- Finally, take time to meditate and feel the balance of the rebirth within yourself.

3. May Day - Beltane

Mayday represents the beginning of the long days of the summer season. It is considered a holy day in Irish and Celtic culture. Beltane was considered a time to celebrate, especially through bonfires and extravagant feasts. This was a very special day for the Celts, one when the veils between the worlds was thinnest. Beltane symbolized a time to celebrate life and included huge feasts, festivals, and fairs.

Historic Celtic Rituals

Celtic tradition believed the time of Beltane welcomes the season of harvest and was considered the most important throughout the year. Although the season involved many rituals and customs, most were associated with fire, so this festival was sometimes called the Celtic fire festival. Ancient rituals included the following:

- One, two, or several huge bonfires were lit as a symbol of life and celebration.

- The flames, ash, and smoke were declared sacred, and people and cattle would walk around the flames for protection, wealth, and health.

- Animal blood was used as a sacrifice, and milk and honey were poured across thresholds to be found by fairies.

- An integral part of the festival was the Beltane feast. Although not as extravagant as the other festivals, it still held significance.

Modern Celebrations

Although the traditional festivities have largely died out in the modern pagan world, the fire festival has been enjoying a revival over the past few years. Neopagans and Wicca groups come together to celebrate the May Day festivities on weekends or hold fairs on weekdays. While the activities and rituals might have changed over time, the sentiment behind this festival remains the same, which is to welcome summer and hope for good fortune.

- Beltane is a fertility festival, so an altar setup symbolizes rebirth and celebration of life.

- The tradition of a maypole dance has been around for a long time and is still prevalent in many pagan cultures. The maypole celebration usually occurs after sunrise, the day after the fire festival.

- Bonfire ritual to celebrate fire and fertility is done in groups to celebrate the love partners have for each other.

- The Beltane planting rite is perfect for a solitary celebration and is a simple rite that celebrates the fertility of the planting season.

Handfasting Ritual

Today many pagan cultures follow handfasting ceremonies instead of traditional weddings, usually done during May Day celebrations. It can be a simple ceremony without the benefit of a state license. Many people also prefer jumping the broom, which is another non-conventional pagan wedding rite.

4. Midsummer - Summer Solstice

The summer solstice occurs when the sun hits the axial tilt of the earth, or in simple words, it's the longest day of the year, i.e., June 21st. This day celebrates light and sun and is closely associated with herbs, flowers, and candles. The Celts dedicated this day to their Celtic goddess, who went by many names. The day is marked and celebrated as the first day of summer.

Historic Celtic Rituals

The Celts had many beliefs regarding the summer solstice and considered the day of utmost importance for many rituals and spells. The Celts believed the sun's power would help banish darkness and evil and, in turn, open gates for an abundance of wealth. The sun was associated with vibrancy, warmth, and light, and the following rituals took place during the historic Celtic periods.

- Numerous bonfires were lit around which lovers danced and jumped over for luck.

- Wheels of fire were cascaded downhills as a symbol of light spreading.

- Delicious feasts were prepared, and people danced around the bonfires for the Druids.

Modern Celebrations

Although much of the old culture surrounding the summer solstice has faded, many people still come together to celebrate the summer solstice with great fervor. These prominently include the pagans, neopagans, Wiccans, and other cultures. Midsummer festivals all over the world include maypole dancing, mountaintop bonfires, and other rituals.

Midsummer Herb Ritual

You can use herbs in numerous ways in pagan summer rituals. Herbs represent nature and have significant power in healing and soothing. Beyond cooking with herbs, you can also turn them into incense or make relaxing candles. Here are some of the best herbs for summer solstice or midsummer rituals and spells.

- Fennel

- Lily

- Chickweed

- Frankincense

- Lavender

- Heather

- Rose

- Vervain

- Mugwort

5. Lughnasa

Lughnasa (August 1st) marked the beginning of the harvest season for ancient Celtic people and celebrated joyously to represent growth and celebration. Due to the joy of an abundant harvest, Celtic people would light bonfires and celebrate the oncoming of a full season. It was considered a time of gratitude or thanksgiving.

Historic Celtic Rituals

For the Celts, Lughnasa celebrates the fruition of the year's harvests and represents the harvest festival of the Celtic culture. In ancient tradition, the Celtic harvest festival used to last a month, with the festivities starting from mid-July and lasting two weeks into august. An old custom was to pick the ripe apples first to make a celebratory drink for the festival. Other Lughnasa rituals included:

- Bilberries (Blueberries) were collected first to gauge the crops' yield. If the blueberries were bountiful, so would the crops be.

- Garlands of flowers and greenery were placed around holy wells dedicated to patron saints.

- A feast containing seasonal fruits and vegetables and baked bread was prepared and enjoyed.

Modern Celebrations

Although Lughnasa celebrations have faded, and it's the least recognized of all the Celtic holidays, Lughnasa festivals and fairs still take place annually in the open-air museum of Craggaunowen. Many pagans celebrate this festival today with bonfires, feasts, and dancing.

6. Autumnal/Fall Equinox

Similar to the spring equinox or St Patrick's Day, the autumn or fall equinox celebrates the balance brought with the day and night of equal length. This sacred day falls around September 21st, somewhere in the middle of the fall season. It is considered a time of harvest, where people come together to gather, store, and preserve their food for the upcoming winter season. According to Celtic traditions, this time holds significant value for rituals and spell-work because of the changing of seasons.

Historic Celtic Rituals

The autumn equinox, known as the second harvest, brings either joy or suffering, depending on the outcome of a farmers' crops. The autumnal equinox brings a pause between autumn and winter seasons, considered the dark season among the Celtic culture. The following rituals were practiced during the fall equinox.

- According to Chinese tradition, the autumn equinox was celebrated with a moonlit dinner after successfully harvesting rice and wheat crops.

- Many people meditated before sunrise to find the balance an equinox might bring into their lives.

- Sustenance through foraging was an important part of the Celtic culture and was usually done during the autumn equinox in preparation for the oncoming winter.

- The ancient Mabon ritual included a bonfire festival to honor the changing season and celebrate the successful harvest.

Modern Celebrations

Modern celebrations during the autumn equinox are based on the same principles and beliefs in ancient teachings. Gratitude campfires, fall foraging hikes, and sunrise yoga meditation are all examples of modern pagan celebrations of the fall equinox.

7. Samhain

Samhain was when where spirits could cross the veil between the living and the dead and communicate with them as possible. Falling on November 1st, Samhain is a fascinating Celtic holiday. Paired with the spooky Halloween, it is considered the beginning of the darker half of the year.

Historic Celtic Rituals

During Samhain, many Celtic rituals that took place were to ward off evil spirits, while the ancestors of a family were invited and honored. Feasts were prepared for the living and the dead. People wore masks and disguised themselves as evil spirits to ward off danger. Essentially, this is where Halloween originated from.

Modern Celebrations

Modern Samhain pagan celebrations include setting up a Samhain altar, making an ancestors' altar, visiting a cemetery, holding a séance to communicate with the dead, finding divinatory guidance through tarot cards, or using Samhain herbs and spices for spells and rituals.

8. Winter Solstice

This is the shortest day of the year (pretty much the opposite of the summer solstice) and is around December 21st. It's considered a time of rebirth where people celebrate by attending festivals, gatherings, or performing rituals. While historic rituals include bonfires and spell-work, modern pagan rituals usually take place at a popular winter solstice site, i.e., the Newgrange burial chamber.

Chapter 10: Spells and Charms

While black magic is believed to cause suffering to other people, "white witchcraft" keeps danger at bay, cures diseases, and grants luck. This chapter discusses different Celtic, Irish, Scottish, and Druid spells. Other spells are used for healing, charms to attract fortune, beauty spells, love, and romance.

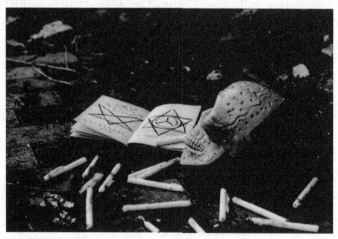

Spells to Attract Good Fortune

At some point, we all aspire to attract good fortune in life, and since we usually attribute bad luck to evil spells, we need good spells to counter that. Performing this spell involves a candle, some string, and a trinket.

First, you want to loop the string through the trinket and then tie it. Swing the trinket above the flame of your candle and chant, asking for good energy.

Repeat this three times and wear the necklace around your neck. The spell will give you a lot more power when you continuously do this.

Irish Beauty Spell

This spell is believed to make you prettier than you ever imagined. You will need a mirror, a pink candle, or incense for this spell. When there is a full moon, take a mirror and go outside or open the window and ensure the moon reflects in the mirror. Take an image of anything you want to improve and place it in the mirror.

Now, say, "Moonshine, Starlight, let the wind carry your light, let your glow cover my body, and let your shine cover every eye." Like most spells, you need to focus on what you want for it to work, which in this case would be the part of you that you'd like to change. Do that, and repeat the incantation three times.

Next, say the following three times, "Moonshine, Starlight, shape and mold my body, as a rose is granted beauty, let me blossom in your light, the light that brings me beauty, and grant me beauty three times three."

When you're done, light a pink candle or incense.

Spell to Recover Stolen Goods

Losing any valuable possession can be devastating, especially when it's stolen. No one wants to lose their hard-earned belongings since they may be difficult to replace. That's where this spell comes in.

1. Take two keys and place them in a sieve, crossways.

2. Have two people have to hold the sieve.

3. Make a cross sign on the suspected thief's forehead, calling their name aloud three times.

4. If the person you suspect is guilty, the keys will be around the sieve. If they're innocent, they won't move at all.

You can take appropriate measures to recover your stolen items when this happens. However, be careful to avoid false accusations since this may impact your relationship with others.

Four Leaf Clover Charm for Luck

Who hasn't heard of the lucky four-leaf clover? These four leaves are rare and are rumored to possess mystical powers representing positive attributes. The Celts believed in their powers and attributed them to hope, faith, love, and luck. Other people believe the four clover leaves will bring wealth, fame, faithful love, and health.

The four leaves are a genetic mutation and very rare, and only about one plant in 10 000 leaves carry the lucky leaves. While getting the leaves for the lucky charms can be challenging, there are different crafts you can use in their place. For instance, buy jewelry designed to symbolize the four clover leaves. It will give you the same results if used properly.

Charm against Danger

When men went into battle, they needed protection against dangers, such as injury, being captured by the enemy, or drowning. Different colored strings were used alongside a mixture of rhymes to evoke cures. The chords were believed to have powers to protect the fighters against harm. If you are going on a mission that could meet some challenges, you need this charm for protection.

Charms to Cure Sicknesses

These were usually administered by what were known as the "wise women" or "wise men." The "knowledge" from these wise people was a charm that could be used to cure ailments in man or animal – things like bruises, toothache, and the sort. The wise person would recite a chant over the sufferer, as well as over the water that would be sprinkled on them or drunk. If you sought the help of the "wise woman," you were not allowed to talk to anyone afterward until they reached home. There were a few other rules attached to this. Going to bed before sunset, no reading, no meat on the day the charm was administered.

Bond of Trust

An interesting custom in Ireland was for men to use their hair and braid it as a bracelet. This would then be presented to the woman they loved as a gift representing trust. For the binding powers of the spell to actually work, the woman needed to accept the gift. Basically, you can't force this spell on someone without their knowing of it or accepting it. This particular spell meant that the parties involved agreed to form a lasting union. When you use this spell, its main purpose is to give you focus and strength to achieve your aims and to make your intentions known.

Irish Charm for Money

Many people aspire to have a fortune of money in their lives. In Irish tradition, it is believed that a black rooster's feather coupled with a gold-colored coin can bring great fortune. You need to hold the coin and feather and go to the crossing points consisting of three fairy paths and call the name of the Goddess Aine three times. This charm will bring you everlasting prosperity, and you will always have money for various purposes. Also, use the charm to solve financial problems you may encounter.

Lucky Horseshoe Charms

Since the 10th century, this tradition continues to be used as a symbol of luck to this very day. You can usually see them over a door where they're meant to bring good fortune into homes and keep bad luck out. The horseshoe is commonly used in different cultures, although there are some disagreements about how it should be hung on the door.

There's a little discrepancy in terms of how to hang the horseshoe. A vast majority believe it should be facing upwards, in a sense collecting and capturing good luck. There is also the notion that it should hang downwards so luck can pour over anyone passing beneath it. Either way, it's believed that the horseshoe possesses luck because blacksmiths were able to bend any material provided by God. The talisman also makes a perfect wedding gift since it symbolizes the tradition of long-standing and is often presented to the bride. A horseshoe was also believed to represent a crescent moon, making it a very potent fertility charm.

Lucky Number Seven Charm

In many cultures, the number 7 is considered lucky and represents perfection and knowledge. This is mainly because of its special mathematical properties. The square and triangle are considered "perfect forms," and the number 7 is a combination of the four sides of the square and the three of the triangle. Hence, perfection. Seven is also significant in many other cases:

- How many days are there in a week?

- How many visible planets are there?

- How many colors does a rainbow have?

That's right, seven. Now all you have to do is involve seven in whatever you want to achieve. For example, seven can act as your winning number the next time you're out betting. Maybe create a charm with seven lucky symbols, like crystals.

Healing Charms

While many charms and spells are specifically meant for practices related to luck, protection against evil spells, love, and romance, others are used for healing different conditions. The following are examples of charms believed to possess healing properties.

A Cure for Mental Health Issues

This treatment should be performed on Thursdays only. The patient sits atop a gray horse and is taken for a ride where the animal gallops at its fastest speed three times around a boundary mark. They will move to an immovable stone where the patient will be asked to speak to the stone. This is the healing procedure, and afterward, it is believed the victim will recover. The process is based on the belief in the powers of the gods that will remove evil spirits causing the mental health challenge.

Irish Charm to Heal Depression

When someone becomes low and experiencing depression, they are said to have a "fairy blast." It is treated by pouring blast water over the victim. A fairy doctor will pour the water, while chanting in praise of the gods with the power to heal the condition. If water is left after performing the procedure, it must be poured into the fire. The entire healing system is based on religious beliefs and invoking the powers of the deities.

Evil Eye Charms

This charm is not as evil as the name suggests but offers protection to the wearer from persons with distrustful eyes. It can guard against negative forces coming from people believed to possess negative eyes. The evil eye charm functions by diverting any harmful intent caused by the harmful eyes when they look into your face. It acts as a protective amulet – the belief being that evil can only be harmful if it looks directly into your eyes.

The eye charm tricks the evil forces so they do not harm you. Most protective eye charms are worn, placed in homes, or carried in a pocket. The charms are also used to guard corporations and individuals against financial losses caused by poor business dealings. Consider this charm if you want to enjoy general protection against evil forces.

While black magic is believed to be harmful, white witchcraft is used to benefit different people. For instance, spells and charms are utilized for various purposes such as luck, healing, love, and romance. However, you need to consult a knowledgeable practitioner for insight into various spells to resolve your challenges. Like in any other religion, these charms and spells are based on belief systems.

Appendix: Glossary of Magical Symbols

Now that we have covered everything about Celtic magic and the Druids, we end this book with some of the most important Celtic symbols, their meanings, and uses. The Celtic symbols hugely influenced how the ancient Celts lived their lives. To this day, these symbols are associated with their culture and Ireland. Even if you don't know much about these symbols or their meanings, you are probably familiar with them. You have seen them somewhere, like in a movie, TV show, or you own a piece of jewelry with a symbol on it, but you don't know what it means. Understanding these magical symbols will make performing spells and rituals a lot easier.

Unfortunately, the exact meaning behind some Celtic symbols will never be known to us because they were not documented. However, many have been interpreted due to their popularity and our curiosity. When it comes to symbols, notice that there are several recurring themes, including but not limited to love, strength, unity, and, of course, loyalty. Also, the number three is incorporated in many symbols because of the Celts' beliefs that all essential things come in threes.

The Meaning behind Celtic Symbols

The Ailm

The Ailm symbol, like the Dora Knot discussed later, represents strength. Although the design behind each symbol is different, the meaning is the same. This symbol is taken from the first letter of the Celtic Ogham alphabet, where the Ailm is supposed to be a tree called the silver fir tree. According to ancient Celts, it was associated with healing one's soul.

The Celts believed that the trees represented strength, and for a good reason. For instance, the oak tree can grow and survive in extremely harsh conditions for hundreds of years. The Ailm symbolizes purification, fertility, strength, health, and healing. It is considered one of the most important Celtic symbols. Nowadays, many brands use it since it promotes many positive notions.

The Awen

Awen is a Celtic word meaning essence or inspiration. There is more than one interpretation of this symbol's representation. Some believe the three lines on the Awen represent the mind, body, and spirit, or earth, sea, and air, or love, wisdom, and truth. It is also believed to have represented the three pillars of awakening:

- Understanding the truth.

- Loving the truth.

- Maintaining the truth.

According to the NeoDruids, a person won't proclaim the truth if they aren't awakened. Nowadays, this symbol is popular since it is used in tattoos, artwork, and jewelry.

The Bowen Knot

The Bowen knot was created in the 17th century and is often called the knot of true love. The knot consists of tangled loops without a beginning or an end. Although this symbol has different variations, the pattern is always the same, with endless loops. The Bowen Knot represents devotion.

The Celtic Bull

The Celtic bull is known for its strength, and it played a significant role in ancient Celtic mythology. The relationship between strong animals and powerful warriors was depicted in Celtic myths. Additionally, animals were included in everything like clothing, carving, and jewelry. The ancient Celts believed that every animal had its virtues, like the bull that was fearless and strong. Bulls also symbolize fertility in women. In addition to strength and fertility, the bull represented wealth. To this day, many people attribute the bull to strength, and why many people choose it for a tattoo.

The Celtic Cross

The Celtic cross is one of the most common and popular Celtic symbols. Since it is a cross, many people have associated it with Christianity. However, this symbol has been around for centuries before Christianity. There are different theories as to what the four arms of the cross represent. Some believe they represent the four elements of earth, fire, air, and water. Another theory says the four arms represent the four sides of the earth, being the north, east, west, and south, while there is another theory that says the arms represent mind, body, heart, and soul. It is also believed that the cross represents the four seasons of the year; winter, spring, summer, and fall, or the stages of the day; morning, midday, evening, and midnight.

There are different theories and legends about the origin of the Celtic cross. Although the cross predates Christianity, one of the legends regarding its origin suggests that either St Declan or St Patrick introduced the cross to Ireland. It is believed that it was created for converting Druids. According to another theory, the Celtic cross is inspired by the ancient Celts Sun Cross. This symbol is still widely popular and used by many people as it is believed it will protect whoever wears it from dark forces and bring them wisdom.

The Celtic Five-Fold

You may not have heard about the Celtic Five-Fold symbol since it isn't as popular online as the other symbols. However, it is everywhere. For instance, the Olympics rings are a variant of this symbol. There are various interpretations as to its representation. Some believe it represents the four directions: north, south, east, and west. Others believe it represents the four seasons: summer, winter, spring, and autumn, while there is another belief that it represents the four elements: earth, air, water, and fire, or god, faith, spirituality, and heaven. The fifth ring is what connects us to the universe.

The Celtic Knotwork

The Celtic Knotwork is another old symbol that originated during the ancient Celts. However, we don't know much about how it came to be. It is believed this symbol can bring health, wealth, and good fortune. Nowadays, people use it in decor and tattoos.

The Circular Knots

The circular knot is considered one of the most important symbols for the Celtics. The circle symbolizes inner life, infinity, and the sun.

The Claddagh Ring

A strong symbol of unity, the Claddagh Ring consists of two hands (friendship) holding a heart (everlasting love) wearing a crown (loyalty). You will find this symbol on many items, but the most common place is on rings.

The name of the ring is derived from "An Cladach," an Irish word meaning flat stony shore. It is the Irish village where the ring was first designed.

The Dara Knot

The Dara Knot is considered one of the most beautiful Celtic symbols. Dara is derived from the Irish word Doire, an oak tree that the Celts and Druids considered sacred and whose roots are represented by the symbol's knots.

The Dara Knot symbolizes strength, wisdom, power, destiny, community, connection, and leadership. During troubled times, the Celts would seek its help for wisdom and strength. This symbol was considered a spiritual charm and also used for decorations. The Dara Knot has become very popular in the last few years and is now used in tattoos, jewelry, and clothes.

The Double Spiral

The double spiral represents the duality of life, death, nature, and balance. For this reason, it often represents things like the equinox (the one day of the year when the day and night have the same duration) as well as how opposites complement each other like life and death, the sun and moon, femininity, and masculinity, yin and yang and light and darkness.

The Dragon

The Celtic dragon is considered invincible, and it represents eternity and wholeness. The Celtic dragon has a sharp arrow on its tail, symbolizing mortality and energy.

The Druid Sigil

The Druid Sigil represents Mother Earth and fertility. The sigils were used during magical rituals, but only a few people used them, and the rituals were kept a secret.

The Eternity Knot

The Celtic eternity knot has three loops since three is considered an important number for the Celtics, and they build everything around it. It is one of the popular Celtic symbols representing immortality, beauty, and eternal youth.

The Green Man

This symbol consists of the head of a man surrounded by leaves. This man has different names, like the man in the tree and Jack O' the Green. He represents rebirth and life and the relationship between man and nature. It is considered one of the oldest Celtic symbols since it dates back to 400 BC and is part of ancient Celtic culture. This symbol is still popular today, as you will find it on many religious buildings. Additionally, it is now regarded as a symbol of the environment.

The Griffin

The griffin is a symbol of nobility, balance, and loyalty. It is a combination of an animal's power and intelligence, represented as a mythical creature with a lion's body and eagle's head.

The Motherhood Knot

You have probably noticed by now how the Celts incorporated various knots into their style and decoration. The Motherhood Knot, obvious by the name, represents the relationship between a mother and child. This symbol transcends any belief or faith since it shows the unbreakable bond and everlasting love between a mother and child, which exists regardless of faith.

The Quaternary Knot

The Quaternary Knot is four-sided and has many interpretations of what it symbolizes. It can either represent the four seasons: summer, winter, spring, and fall, the four directions: north, south, east, and west, the four elements; earth, water, air, and fire, or the four Celtic festivals; Samhain, Imbolc, Beltane, and Lughnasadh. Nowadays, many people opt for this symbol as a tattoo.

The Sailor's Knot

Since sailors would spend weeks or months at sea, the sailor's knot is a symbol of endless love, separation, and parting. This symbol was probably originated by sailors who left these knots for their loved ones at home, so they would remember them when separated for extended periods.

The Serch Bythol

The Serch Bythol represents everlasting love. The word itself means everlasting love in Welsh and is considered a Celtic symbol for the family. It consists of two triskeles joined together to form a circle representing eternity. The three arcs of the triskele symbolize the mind, body, and spirit. This symbol proves the ancient Celts had a profound understanding of their feelings, emotions, and relationships. Since it has a deep beautiful meaning, many people choose to incorporate this symbol in jewelry and as a gift.

The Shamrock

"I'll seek a four-leaved shamrock in all thy fairy dells, and if I find the charmed leaves, oh, how I'll weave my spells." Samuel Lover.

One of the first things that come to mind when we think of Ireland is the shamrock. Nowadays, the symbol is associated with St Patrick's Day celebration and good luck. It is believed that St Patrick used the shamrock to explain the Holy Trinity's unity and convert pagans to Christianity. However, the shamrock's origins go way back to the Celtic culture and are symbolic of the Druids. They believed the leaves of this plant symbolized the triad. Since, as we have mentioned, they believed all important things in life come in three.

They believed that it served as protection from evil, bad eyes, and bad words, and the shamrock would warn them of a storm by standing in an upright position. The shamrock is supposed to represent good luck and fortune, something many people in and outside of Ireland still believe. It is also the national flower of the country.

The Shillelagh

The Shillelagh is a short wooden club that was used to settle disputes, made from blackthorn wood or oak.

Solomon's Knot

This symbol was named after King Solomon and represented strength, wisdom, and masculinity. Usually, people who hope to represent themselves as authoritative or powerful wear this symbol.

The St. Brigid Cross

St Brigid was born in 400 AD in Dundalk. She was the daughter of a Christian woman called Brocca, who St Patrick baptized. Brigid became a nun, and the cross is attributed to her. It is believed that she created this cross after a dying pagan that wanted to be baptized, but some believed to be her father. However, it is also associated with the life-giving goddess, who also goes by the name Brigid and belongs to the Tuatha de Danann, a supernatural race in Irish mythology. The cross is usually used during the beginning of the spring celebrations and the festival of the goddess Brigid occurring simultaneously. The Irish hang this cross in their houses to protect them from fires and evil spirits.

The Tree of Life

The tree of life has always been associated with the Druids. They believe the earth and heaven are connected, and the tree of life represents this connection. According to the ancient Celts, it is a symbol of wisdom, strength, and long life. The tree also represents harmony and balance. The Celts considered trees a symbol of rebirth since they associated rebirth with how the trees change every season. Additionally, they considered trees the spirits of their ancestors. Trees were so sacred to the Celts, especially the oak tree, they would hold important meetings under them. They believed the tree of life was a doorway to the land of the fairies, and it protected their lands against enemies. Nowadays, this symbol is used in many jewelry pieces, as it is very popular.

The Triquetra

The Triquetra is also known as the Trinity Knot. The word Triquetra is Latin and means three-cornered. This symbol has been around ever since the Iron Age, and you can find it in Irish architecture, art, and design today. This symbol represents the three stages of the neopagan goddess's life; as a virgin, mother, and wise woman. Some Celts considered this symbol to represent earth, fire, and water, while others considered it a representation of the earth, sea, and the sky. The Triquetra is also called the Irish Love Knot and symbolizes eternal love. This knot also represents eternal spiritual life without a beginning or an end.

Not much is known regarding the origins of this symbol, but some believe it was inspired by the lunar and solar cycles. If you think this symbol looks familiar, then you aren't wrong. This symbol is everywhere today in jewelry and illustrations, and if you saw the original TV show, Charmed, it was drawn on the "Book of Shadows," they used for spells.

The Triskelion

The Triskelion, or the Triskele, reflects the Celts' belief that all-important things come in threes. The name of this symbol is derived from the Greek word Triskeles, meaning three legs, or the third time's the charm, something we still say today. It is believed the Triskelion has been around since the Neolithic era. The symbol consists of 3 clockwise spirals and is one of the oldest symbols known to man. The three spirals signify the earth or harmony. However, if the spirals are anti-clockwise, they are believed to be pagan symbols that control and manipulate nature. Since the spirals look as if they are moving, they signify moving forward and defeating hardships. They can also symbolize progress and strength.

The Wheel of Taranis

Taranis is the Celtic god of thunder, and he is the brother of the Roman god of thunder, Jupiter. They are portrayed as bearded heroes holding lighting and a wheel in their hands. According to Celtic mythology, Taranis united the lighting, sky, and the sun.

The Celtics have a rich and fascinating history, and their symbols represent it exceptionally well. These symbols are thousands of years old, and that they still intrigue people is proof of how great their culture was. Not only do these symbols look beautiful, which is why they are incorporated in buildings, designs, jewelry, and clothes, but they also have beautiful meanings making them even more fascinating.

Beautiful meanings like everlasting love and loyalty make it seem like these symbols are out of a fairy tale. Irish culture is extremely famous for its mythology, and they introduced many mythical creatures we are very familiar with, like fairies and mermaids.

There is something very beautiful, mysterious, and enchanting about the Celts and their culture, especially since there are so many things we still don't know, making them all the more intriguing.

Conclusion

When you first become interested, Celtic magic, plant shamanism, paganism, Druidry, and other ideas within European folklore seem quite intimidating and even aimless. However, armed with the principles outlined in this book, together with the numerous techniques and strategies we have covered, you have everything you need to dive deep into this sea of knowledge and discover a new world.

The most challenging part of the entire process is going through the exercises and determining how you perform in the real world. If you come from a spiritual background and have some training in meditation or yoga, that knowledge will certainly help you during this process. For those completely new, it might be challenging to get in touch with your feelings and thoughts and understand how you channel different parts of the process. Most newcomers to this field will constantly argue among themselves about whether or not it is working or whether or not they are feeling the right sensations. You must understand there is no clear right or wrong. It is not about getting to the finish line first. It is about being true to yourself and developing as a person.

The various things we covered about the Irish people and their unique heritage are not limited to that region, religion, or race. These are universal concepts that can be applied by anyone, anywhere in the world. It will definitely help if you have the resources mentioned in this book at your disposal, but there are many things specific to this region. However, there are different ways to work around this, and with the interconnected world today, it should be no problem to get your hands on the things you need.

The most important thing to note is the time you invest in this practice. This is not a degree that will take several years. The elder Druids in the Celtic culture spent an entire lifetime perfecting their specialization. Students weren't considered masters even after twenty years of being a master's disciple. The various colored robes were not achieved by spending a certain amount of time but awarded when students showed mastery of their work and thought of the greater good.

The purpose of Druidry and the various shamanistic practices was to bring about good, starting with the individual who practiced it and slowly spreading it to the world around them, including everything tangible and intangible. In reality, we can only be happy when we are c0ntent with everything inside and out. By going through these practices and lessons and complimenting them with research, you will develop a higher level of consciousness to enlighten you and allow you to see things from a holistic view. With this guide by your side, you are well on your way to developing a happier, healthier life.

Here's another book by Mari Silva that you might like

MARI SILVA

CEREMONIAL MAGICK

UNLOCKING RITUAL MAGICK,
THE HISTORY OF LEARNED MAGIC,
AND SECRETS OF OCCULTISM

Your Free Gift (only available for a limited time)

Thanks for getting this book! If you want to learn more about various spirituality topics, then join Mari Silva's community and get a free guided meditation MP3 for awakening your third eye. This guided meditation mp3 is designed to open and strengthen ones third eye so you can experience a higher state of consciousness. Simply visit the link below the image to get started.

https://spiritualityspot.com/meditation

References

Cartwright, M. (2021a). Ancient Celtic Religion. World History Encyclopedia.

https://www.worldhistory.org/Ancient_Celtic_Religion

Cartwright, M. (2021b). Ancient Celts. World History Encyclopedia.

https://www.worldhistory.org/celt/

Duffy, K. (2000). Who were the Celts? Barnes & Noble.

Jarus, O. (2014, April 7). History of the Celts. Livescience.Com; Live Science.

https://www.livescience.com/44666-history-of-the-celts.html

May, A. (2019, November 14). Celtic Wicca - myths and secrets explained. Welcome To Wicca

Now. https://wiccanow.com/celtic-wicca-myths-and-secrets-explained

Putka, S. (2021, June 4). The ancient Celts: Iron age foes of Rome who left behind more than

weapons. Discover Magazine.

https://www.discovermagazine.com/planet-earth/the-ancient-celts-iron-age-foes-of-rome-who-left-behind-more-than-weapons

Flanagan, K. (2020, February 13). Aengus Óg: The Irish god of love. The Brehon Academy. https://brehonacademy.org/aengus-og-the-irish-god-of-love

God Studies: Cernunnos. (n.d.). Sabrina's Grimoire. Retrieved from https://sabrinasgrimoire.tumblr.com/post/622301491987906560/god-studies-cernunnos

Goddess epona. (2012, June 13). Journeying to the Goddess. https://journeyingtothegoddess.wordpress.com/2012/06/13/goddess-epona

Info. (2020, February 11). Ogma: The god of speech & language. Order of Bards, Ovates &

Druids. https://druidry.org/resources/ogma-the-god-of-speech-language

Lugh. (n.d.). Wiccaneopagan.Com. Retrieved from http://www.wiccaneopagan.com/group/deities/forum/topics/2453436:Topic:59053

Mainyu, E. A. (Ed.). (2011). Belenus. Aud Publishing.

Mandal, D. (2018, July 2). 15 ancient Celtic gods and goddesses you should know about. Realm

of History. https://www.realmofhistory.com/2018/07/02/ancient-celtic-gods-goddesses-facts

Mantrik. (2013, August 27). Introduction to Belenos. Wyrdfyre. https://belinus1.wordpress.com/2013/08/27/introduction-to-belinus

The Editors of Encyclopedia Britannica. (2017). Danu. In Encyclopedia Britannica.

The Editors of Encyclopedia Britannica. (2018). Belenus. In Encyclopedia Britannica.

Treanor, D., Elle, Walker, R., Roots, S., Fields, K., Duff, C., Latta, A. L., 30+ Types of Fairies Worldwide: Brownies, Elves, Gnomes, and More!, Celtic Deities: 10 Lesser-Known Celtic Gods and Goddesses,

Tavernier, M., Are Fairies Real? Origins and Evidence that Fairies Exist, & Triple Goddess: Maiden, Mother, and Crone for Modern Practitioners. (2020, April 10). Celtic Goddess of War: 8 ways to work with The Morrigan. Otherworldly Oracle.

https://otherworldlyoracle.com/celtic-goddess-of-war

Wigington, P. (n.d.-a). Cernunnos, the wild Celtic god of the Forest. Learn Religions. Retrieved from https://www.learnreligions.com/cernunnos-wild-god-of-the-forest-2561959

Wigington, P. (n.d.-b). The Dagda, the father god of Ireland. Learn Religions. Retrieved from https://www.learnreligions.com/the-dagda-father-god-of-ireland-2561706

Zuberbuehler, A. (1996). Fieldstones. Players Press.

Aos Sí – ancestors of Ireland. (2021, June 7). Symbol Sage. https://symbolsage.com/aos-si-ancestors-of-ireland/

Irish Pagan beliefs. (2018, September 25). Lora O'Brien - Irish Author & Guide.

https://loraobrien.ie/irish-pagan-beliefs

Metalgaia. (2012, June 6). Why Wicca and Celtic Paganism are different things. Metal Gaia. https://metal-gaia.com/2012/06/06/why-wicca-and-celtic-paganism-are-different-things

Paganism in Scotland. (n.d.). Electricscotland.Com. Retrieved from https://electricscotland.com/bible/paganism.htm

Scott. (2017, April 24). Who the hell is Sidhe? – Fairy Faith and Animism in Scotland. A Challenge to Divinity. Cailleach's Herbarium. https://cailleachs-herbarium.com/2017/04/who-the-hell-is-sidhe-fairy-faith-and-animism-in-scotland-a-challenge-to-divinity

Scottish folklore - Cat Sìth & Cù-Sìth. (n.d.). Timberbush-Tours.Co.Uk. Retrieved from https://www.timberbush-tours.co.uk/news-offers/scottish-folklore-cat-sith-cu-sith

The Newsroom. (2016, March 31). The tale of Scottish banshees: Baobhan Sith. The Scotsman. https://www.scotsman.com/whats-on/arts-and-entertainment/tale-scottish-banshees-baobhan-sith-1479692

The tuatha D' danann - Ireland's greatest tribe. (n.d.). IrelandInformation.Com. Retrieved from https://www.ireland-information.com/irish-mythology/tuatha-de-danann-irish-legend.html

Dana. (n.d.). invoking awen – The Druid's Garden. The Druid's Garden. Retrieved from https://druidgarden.wordpress.com/tag/invoking-awen

Druids of California. (n.d.). CaliforniaDruids.Org. Retrieved from https://californiaDruids.org/pages/history.html

Former Student. (2019, July 18). Modern-day Druids: No animal sacrifices, but connected to community, history. Cronkite News - Arizona PBS. https://cronkitenews.azpbs.org/2019/07/18/modern-Druids-arizona

Info. (2019a, November 27). Bard. Order of Bards, Ovates & Druids. https://druidry.org/druid-way/what-druidry/what-is-a-bard

Info. (2019b, November 27). Druid. Order of Bards, Ovates & Druids. https://druidry.org/druid-way/what-druidry/what-is-a-druid

Info. (2019c, November 27). Ovate. Order of Bards, Ovates & Druids. https://druidry.org/druid-way/what-druidry/what-is-an-ovate

Philip. (2019, November 21). Groups & groves. Order of Bards, Ovates & Druids. https://druidry.org/get-involved/groups-groves

Philip. (2020, March 16). The three functions of druidry. Order of Bards, Ovates & Druids. https://druidry.org/resources/the-three-functions-of-druidry

Rule of Awen. (n.d.). Aoda.Org. Retrieved from https://aoda.org/aoda-structure/gnostic-celtic-church-gcc/rule-of-awen

Shedding light on Stonehenge and the summer solstice. (2020, June 17). VisitBritain. https://www.visitbritain.com/au/en/media/story-ideas/shedding-light-stonehenge-and-summer-solstice-0

The order of bards ovates and Druids (OBOD). (2013, May 2). The Druid Network. https://druidnetwork.org/what-is-druidry/learning-resources/obod

All Answers Ltd. (2021, December 31). Trees in Celtic culture and art: An analysis.

Ukessays.Com; UK Essays. https://www.ukessays.com/essays/arts/trees-celtic-culture-art-analysis-3271.php

Hawthorn Tree in Celtic mythology. (2013, September 26). Ireland Calling. https://ireland-calling.com/celtic-mythology-hawthorn-tree

Festivals & Rituals. (n.d.). Retrieved from The Ancient Celtic Relgion website:

http://theancientcelticreligion.weebly.com/-festivals--rituals.html

Info. (2019, November 27). Oracles & divination in druidry. Retrieved from Order of Bards, Ovates & Druids website:

https://druidry.org/druid-way/teaching-and-practice/oracles-divination-druidry

Marketing The Conscious Club. (2019, November 13). Why ceremonies and rituals are still important today —. Retrieved from The Conscious Club website:

https://theconsciousclub.com/articles/2019/10/17/why-ceremonies-and-rituals-are-still-important-today

Ancient Irish spells and charms to celebrate Halloween. (2021, October 9). Retrieved from IrishCentral.com website: https://www.irishcentral.com/roots/ancient-irish-spells-charms

Campsie, A. (2019, October 17). 9 charms, spells, and cures used by Highland witches. The Scotsman. Retrieved from https://www.scotsman.com/heritage-and-retro/heritage/9-charms-spells-and-cures-used-highland-witches-1404985

Cath. (2021, May 4). 11 fascinating Celtic symbols and their meanings. Travel Around Ireland.

https://travelaroundireland.com/celtic-symbols-and-their-meanings

Made in the USA
Monee, IL
15 October 2023

44623669R00077